J. Dunlea.

OXFORD MEDICAL PUBLICATIONS

Good mouthkeeping

Good mouthkeeping

or how to save your children's teeth,
and your own too while you're about it

SECOND EDITION

John Besford

OXFORD NEW YORK TORONTO
OXFORD UNIVERSITY PRESS

1984

Oxford University Press, Walton Street, Oxford OX2 6DP

London New York Toronto
Delhi Bombay Calcutta Madras Karachi
Kuala Lumpur Singapore Hong Kong Tokyo
Nairobi Dar es Salaam Cape Town
Melbourne Auckland

and associated companies in
Beirut Berlin Ibadan Mexico City Nicosia

Oxford is a trade mark of Oxford University Press

First published by Debeli Press, 1980
Second edition, 1984

British Library Cataloguing in Publication Data

Besford, John
Good mouthkeeping.—(Oxford medical publications)
1. Dental caries—Prevention
I. Title
617.6'7052   RK331
ISBN 0–19–261461–4

Library of Congress Cataloging in Publication Data
Besford, John
Good mouthkeeping, or, How to save your children's teeth, and your own too while
you're about it.
(Oxford medical publications)
1. Teeth—Care and hygiene. 2. Nutrition and dental health.   I. Title.
II. Title: Good mouthkeeping.
III. Title: How to save your children's teeth, and
your own too while you're about it. IV. Series.
RK61.B53 1984   617.6'01   84–10069
ISBN 0–19–261461–4 (pbk.)

Printed in Great Britain by
Richard Clay (The Chaucer Press) Ltd.
Bungay, Suffolk

Contents

Acknowledgements

I am grateful to the following people who have helped me with their time and knowledge.

Sheridan Besford – typing
Philip Bristow – sugar in drugs
Ron Brandt – reading and information
Alan Brook – information
Anne Burgess – proof reading
Michael Craft – reading and much advice
Issy Cole-Hamilton – sugar in food and drink
Sara Davies – sugar in baby foods
Phil DeNicolo – U.S. terms
Roy Duckworth – fluoride in tea
Elizabeth Elliott – information and encouragement
Stephen Fisher – terminology
Brenda Fox– terrific support for the first edition
Dorothy Geddes – Stephan curves
Jasmina Hamzavi – reading and punctuation
Martin Hobdell – encouragement
Linda Humphrey – fluoridation
Karen Jeffereys – sugar in spoonfuls
Newell Johnson – caries
Sally Joyston-Bechal – fluoridation
Bernie Kieser – looking for plaque & tying knots
Jenny King – reading and information
Kevin Lewis – preventive dentistry
Sena Narendran – world sugar consumption
John Richards – influence
Graham Roberts – sugar in drugs
Barry Scheer – children's plaque control and fluoride

Ruscha Schorr-Kon – reading and imagination
Stephan Schorr-Kon – suggesting the title
Ted Seal – dental therapists
Bernard Smith – tooth wear
Kate Start – baby foods
Ken Stephen – fluoride
Ron Speirs – fluoride
Pat Sullivan – orthodontics
Roger Sutton – enthusiasm
Sally Verity – dental health education
Peter Warren – biochemistry
Patricia Wright – applied psychology
John Yudkin – sugar

I am specially grateful to **Aubrey Sheiham** and **Sonja Besford**. Aubrey has been unstinting in his supply of references, information, addresses, and advice on the text. Sonja has provided the inspiration, optimism, and hard work necessary to publish the first edition and cajole the second.

Part 1

1

Dental fatalism

Is losing teeth inevitable – a part of growing old? Judging from everyday experience you would have every right to think so, because most older people you meet have lost some teeth and a good many of them have no natural teeth left at all. In the same way, you may think that children are bound to have teeth removed because of decay at one time or another during their childhood, or at least to have fillings.

Yet nowadays, a dentist with young children would be very disappointed if they had any decay at all, or lost any teeth except milk teeth at the proper time.

I say young children because some of the facts about preventing decay have only come to light in recent years, and the combined effects of the various measures against decay are only now being realized. The results of this knowledge are:

DENTAL DECAY CAN BE PREVENTED COMPLETELY
(though not without effort and attention)

IT IS POSSIBLE TO KEEP ALL ONE'S TEETH FOR A LIFETIME
(though not without effort and attention)

The purpose of this book is to explain first how dental disease happens, and secondly how you can banish it altogether, or, if you are too late for that, at least stop it 'dead in its tracks'. The essence of how dental disease happens is well understood, though some of the biochemical details have yet to be mapped out, and the methods by which children can grow up with perfect teeth are known with happy certainty.

What about this 'effort and attention'? As with many things, controlling dental disease is an activity where you don't get something for nothing. That isn't altogether true, because fluoride toothpaste, which most of us now use, gives quite a lot of protection for very little effort, and, if you live in an area with the right amount of fluoride in the water, your children will have half the decay problem solved with no effort at all.

But only half, and the other half requires application. I am going to work on three assumptions. First, that you would want your very young or future children to have no tooth decay. Second, your children who have already had decay to have no more and, third, for both you and your children to keep your permanent teeth for life. To achieve this desirable result you have to apply some mental energy to the situation to understand what causes dental disease and, then, to learn the habits and skills which can control it. Perhaps the problem is more to do with **unlearning** rather than learning. If you have been cleaning your teeth a certain way all your life, it is difficult to lose that habit and replace it with one which requires you to look carefully and concentrate on what you are doing. And, if you have esablished certain eating habits in your home which include frequent sugary snacks, it may be difficult to change those patterns of eating and replace them with more healthy ones.

Babies are at a great advantage because they don't have to unlearn habits. You can start them off by not adding sugar to the food they eat and drink, and by buying food with little sugar in it, so that they don't acquire a hankering for sweet things. Later on, when they begin to brush their own teeth, they can learn from you an effective method from the outset, and that will seem the most normal thing.

Because young children imitate their parents so much, it will probably be necessary for you to do the same things. You can't keep secret caches of chocolates for yourself in your bedroom and not expect your children to ask for sweets. There are no secret places in a home. And, if you show them a way to clean their teeth which takes five minutes, they will not find it convincing if they see you doing a cursory 30-second scrub.

So I have written this book for you to become a dental teacher in your own home, by knowledge and example.

The book has two parts, first the explanations in twelve short chapters, and second an 'information package' to help you choose foods, get more information and talk to your dentist on level terms. The last chapter before the information section is called 'Does losing your teeth matter?' I had difficulty in locating this. Initially I put it where it is now. Then one of my proof readers, a very experienced dental educator, said it must go first, because that is the sensible place to explain the penalties of losing teeth, and increase motivation to save them. This seemed so logical that I wondered why I had placed it at the end. The answer seems to be that I need two 'motivational' sections: one at the beginning to encourage you to read the book and one at the end to encourage you to go and **do** something with your new knowledge. But, on the assumption that you wouldn't buy or borrow this book unless you were interested, I decided to leave it at the end. Those of you who doubt the seriousness of losing teeth can start by reading Chapter 10. In any case, the book is not something which most people will want, or have time, to plough right through from beginning to end. It probably contains too much information to be digested at a sitting, and the order of reading is not crucial.

The information given in this book represents the concensus view of a number of academics and other dental specialists, and is therefore up to date at this moment (June 1984). However, dentistry is developing all the time, and new evidence is continually being collected, which alters opinions. For example, it seems likely that when the new survey of the dental health of children in Britain is published in the mid-1980s, a marked drop in decay rate will be recorded. Already various smaller reports show an annual decline in decay of about 5 per cent in children and 1 per cent in adults. This means that today's children already have only half the decay that children had ten years ago. Fluoride toothpaste may get much of the credit. The forthcoming survey may also show that sugar contents of foods have dropped by public demand, and that more dentists have become committed to preventive dentistry.

By that time, this book ought to be out of print and out of date.

One last point, by way of introduction, is that nobody should pretend that teeth are the most important thing in life though for an unfortunate few they do become just that. My hope is that with knowledge, and the increased confidence which knowledge brings, dental health may be moved a few points up your list of priorities and that you will feel less fatalistic about the inevitability of dental disease. This will save you and your children the pain, anxiety, inconvenience, social embarrassment, and expense which losing teeth, or having dental repair work, can cause and make visits to the dentist less frequent. Does that sound appealing? Read on.

2

What is dental disease?

Roughly speaking, dental disease consists of two components:

TOOTH DECAY – Dentists call this **caries** (a singular noun pronounced 'care is').

GUM DISEASE – Dentists' jargon is **periodontal disease** although some dentists, myself included, use gum disease. An old-fashioned lay term for it is pyorrhoea.

Dentists deal with other problems also, but these two and their consequences occupy most dentists most of the time.

In terms of tooth loss, the more important of these is gum disease. That is to say, more teeth are removed because of gum disease than any other cause. One reason for this is that, while dentists have for decades had quite good techniques for repairing teeth, there is no way of repairing gums. Transplants of pieces of gum and bone to repair losses are carried out in some specialized centres, with encouraging results, but, at the moment, most people who have grown 'long in the tooth' as the result of gum disease will remain so. Another reason for the greater numerical importance of gum disease is that the gum and the tooth socket are the foundations of the tooth. If they break down, no amount of filling of the tooth will save it.

In the lives of children, however, tooth decay is the primary cause of losing teeth early. The reason for this difference is simple. Gum disease is an extremely slow process which, though it may start in children as soon as the teeth come through, usually takes at least thirty years to reach a degree at which teeth are lost. Tooth decay is much faster, say two years, from the first appearance of decay on the tooth surface, to the time when decay has reached the nerve in the middle of the tooth. So while we all know about decay affecting both sets of teeth in children, it is unusual for people to lose teeth through gum disease until their mid-thirties. But from that age onwards gum disease is the main reason for teeth being extracted, and gum disease is, in the end, responsible for the highest number of teeth lost.

BIOLOGICAL VARIATION

Any time one talks about trends like these of dental disease in a population, certain qualifications are necessary before they can be applied to individual people, in particular your child. The trends are based on averages, and your child may or may not be near the average. He or she may have a tendency to more decay or less decay than the average. I said that it takes about two years for a small hole at the surface of the tooth to grow to reach the middle. Well, on average it does, but in your child it might be faster or slower. A survey of children's dental health in Britian was published in 1973 and showed that while 29 per cent of five-year-olds had no decay, this figure dropped to 7 per cent in nine and ten year olds, and to only 3 per cent by the age of fifteen. Today that last figure may be nearer 6 per cent, but, if only six children in a hundred by the age of fifteen have had no decay, it would be unwise to assume that your child (**unaided**) will be one of them. The chances are very much against it. However, if you can do the things recommended in this book, a new baby is very likely to grow up to be among that 6 per cent, and have perfect teeth.

This idea of average trends and departures from the average is called **biological variation** and it is the curse of trying to write about anything to do with health. Eating sugar in foods makes many people fat, but not everybody. Smoking causes heart or lung disease, but not in everyone who smokes. Doing dentistry gives some dentists back trouble, but not all of them. You might know a child who eats lots of sweets and has no decay, but this is unusual. In the UK only **three adults in a thousand** have never had decay.

Information which I give you about risks of dental disease will be 'average' information. It must be modified by you for your particular children in the light of what you can see for yourself. Later on I shall tell you what to look for.

One other point worth mentioning at this stage, is that I believe, with many other dentists, **that what you do about your own and your children's dental health at home is more effective than anything a dentist can do**. I also believe that it is not at all difficult to understand how to take charge of your dental fate. Acting on that information is more difficult, and only you can decide whether it is worth it for yourself. For your children, however, who will be greatly influenced in their early life by what you do and what you show them how to do, it is almost certainly worth the effort.

3

Plaque

An unusual thing has happened in the understanding of dental disease in the last twenty years or so. It has been realized that one substance has to be present on the teeth for dental disease of either type to occur, one substance responsible for two quite different disease processes. That substance is called **plaque** (pronounced either to rhyme with 'black' or with 'park'). This discovery has simplified things considerably, for it is now clear that if you remove plaque from the teeth often enough and completely enough, both decay and gum disease stop.

Unfortunately, many older people were unable to benefit from this knowledge. The classic work showing the relationship between plaque and gum disease was not published until the early 1960s. I was made aware of this one day in 1969 when a dental student asked me a very pointed question. She was treating a cheerful middle-aged lady and she showed me the very thick wad of dental hospital notes about the patient. She said, 'this lady has attended our dental school regularly for treatment since she was a schoolgirl of thirteen; she is now forty-two. Why has she lost so many teeth?' I felt embarrassed. It seemed a very clear-cut failure by us, because the patient appeared to be doing all she could, and I could not answer the question otherwise. Later I saw that by the time the full significance of plaque on the teeth was realized and incorporated into the teaching in our dental schools, this patient was thirty-five and quite a lot of damage had already been done. I now think of dentistry as BP and AP – Before Plaque and After Plaque.

WHAT IS PLAQUE AND HOW DOES IT GET ON TEETH?

In our bodies, and those of other animals, both outer and inner surfaces are covered by bacteria. In most areas these bacteria are harmless, living in peaceful co-existence with the cells of the body surfaces. In many cases they are positively beneficial, because, by competing for space and food, they prevent the attachment and growth of harmful types of bacteria, yeasts, and fungi, which are always present in the environment. Each zone of the body has its own set of conditions, or micro-environment, which favours particular residential bacteria. Before babies are born they are germ-free, but as soon as they reach the outside world, bacteria, mostly from the the mother, colonize their surfaces. In the mouth the warm, wet, and sometimes food-laden conditions favour many different kinds of bacteria, and among them are certain types called **streptococci**. (This rhymes with 'Step-toe' and 'sock-eye' or 'fox-eye' in North America. The latter is phonetically more accurate.) Some kinds of streptococci are responsible for sore throats, scarlet fever, and other illnesses, but the types usually found in the mouth are more peaceful. Certain of these residential streptococci have a special ability to attach themselves to **hard** surfaces. Once there, they settle down to dividing and producing daughter cells over and over again until they have become colonies which are large enough to be seen by the eye. They cannot be seen easily, because the colonies are almost transparent, but, if dyes are used, they stand out as little dots of colour on the tooth surface. These bacteria cannot distinguish between different kinds of hard surface in the mouth – tooth, filling, denture, tartar – any hard surface will do. Other kinds of streptococci live on the soft surface of cheeks, gums, tongue, etc., but it is the hard surface ones which seem to initiate the formation of plaque.

Soon after the pioneering streptococci have formed colonies, other kinds of bacteria attach themselves, including long thin ones which mesh together. Proteins from the saliva are mixed in and the colonies expand and merge together in a kind of micro-urban sprawl. After a few hours the originally clean tooth surface is completely covered by this mixture. The mixture is called plaque.

Note that in the whole of this description, I have scarcely mentioned food. Plaque forms in the presence or absence of food. Many people believe, as dentists did, that the purpose of brushing the teeth is to remove food left over from meals. It is true that some foods stick to the teeth, sweet biscuits for example, but with or without food, plaque is the cause of dental disease and

THE PURPOSE OF CLEANING TEETH IS TO REMOVE PLAQUE NOT FOOD.

Try an experiment with yourself. A few hours after you have cleaned your teeth, but before the next meal, scrape a tooth surface close to the gum with your finger nail and have a look at the nail. You will see that you have collected a small amount of whitish-grey, sticky material – plaque.

SUGAR AND PLAQUE

Although food is not necessary to the formation of plaque, certain foods do make a difference to its composition, namely those foods containing sugar. The streptococci attached to the tooth surface use sugar for energy, with dire consequences to the teeth. But they also turn some of it into sticky substances called **glucans** (polymers of the simplest sugar molecules such as glucose and fructose). These insoluble 'glucan glues' make the plaque thicker, help the bacteria adhere to the hard surfaces and help protect them from being washed off the tooth by the flow of saliva. They may also be converted back to sugar by the bacteria, and then used for energy.

As you can see, plaque is a complicated mixture of things and studying it has occupied hundreds of scientists for many years. The inner layers of plaque are different from the outer. Plaque composition varies in different parts of each tooth and between different teeth, because of slight differences in the micro-environment. Old plaque is different from new plaque. In spite of these variations, it is now absolutely established that tooth decay and gum disease will not occur without the existence of plaque. We shall now consider the first of these, tooth decay, the one which causes most damage in children.

4

Plaque, sugar, and tooth decay

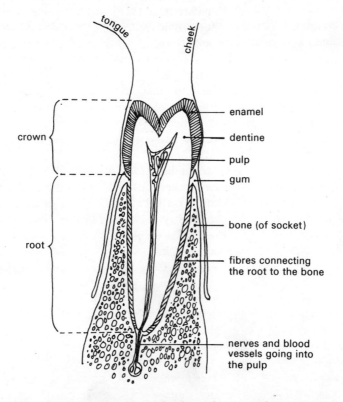

Fig. 1. Cross-section of lower back tooth, etc. to show structure and names.

To understand tooth decay it is necessary to know something about the structure of the tooth. Teeth are formed from two specialized tissues, one of which produces the very

hard **enamel** on the outside of the crown and the other the
not-so-hard **dentine**, on the inside (ivory is the dentine of the
elephant and is similar to human dentine). Both of these
tooth materials gain their hardness from crystals of calcium
salts (mainly calcium hydroxy-apatite) deposited on minute
fibres – the enamel having more crystals and therefore being
harder and more translucent. A few other minerals are
present in minute traces inside the calcium crystals; the
most important of these is fluoride, which will get a chapter
to itself in this book.

Most of the mineral salts are laid down in the teeth before
they erupt through the gum into the mouth, so that the
teeth are hard and strong for chewing straight away. After
the **crowns** of the teeth appear in the mouth, more mineral
salts from the saliva are deposited in the surface layers of the
teeth and they gradually become even harder. Fluoride is
very important in this **secondary mineralization** too, but the
secondary mineralization takes many years to complete.

One feature common to all mineral salts is that they
dissolve in water, even if only slightly. They are said to be
soluble in water. If acid is present their solubility is
increased, and if a lot of acid is present the solubility
increases dramatically. Since teeth are mainly composed of
salts they are particularly prone to attack by acids.

Very striking examples of this are seen in people whose
tooth enamel has worn away, sometimes to the point where
holes are left through which the darker yellow dentine
shows. This spoils the appearance of their teeth and brings
them to the dentist. Enquiry into the histories of these
people usually shows that they have, or used to have, a
chronic condition which caused them to vomit or regurgi-
tate stomach acids. Common examples of this include
anorexia nervosa (and a variant called bulaemia nervosa),
prolonged pregnancy sickness, and alcoholism. They may
also have eaten a lot of citrus fruit – far more than most of us
– or drunk lemon juice every morning. Citric acid from
these fruits has a particular affinity for calcium salts. What

makes it worse is that the people who bring up stomach acid, and the citrus eaters, usually brush their teeth soon afterwards, when the surface crystals are in a delicate state and easily worn away, and before any remineralization can take place. In any case the stomach and citric acids are in contact with the teeth for fairly short periods every day and it takes many years for the enamel to dissolve away.

Tooth decay is also caused by acid attack, which is different from the stomach acid/citrus fruit problem in two ways. First, the acid attack is concentrated at particular sites on the tooth, whereas with lemons, etc., acid washes over the whole tooth surface. Second, the acid attack is greatly prolonged. Both of these differences can be explained by the fact that in decay the acid is produced inside the plaque film. When you brush your teeth, plaque remains in certain areas where the brush cannot reach, and those are the sites where decay is most common. And, being **inside** the plaque, with its insoluble glucans, the acid is protected from being washed away by saliva, unlike the citrus juice or stomach acid.

How is acid produced in plaque?

Many of the bacteria living in the plaque film use sugar, when it's available, as food. It gives them energy for growth, staying alive, producing the glucan glues, and so on. But instead of breaking the sugar all the way down to carbon dioxide and water as our bodies do, many of their breakdown products are acids. These acids build up in concentration in the sticky plaque film, safe from the neutralizing, or 'buffering' effect of saliva, and they are in a perfect position to cause the tooth surface to dissolve, or **demineralize**. This is early tooth decay.

THE STAGES OF TOOTH DECAY

At first only a few crystals are dissolved, and a small zone on

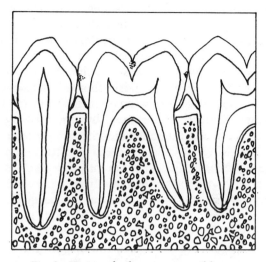

Fig. 2. Very early decay – reversible.

the surface of the enamel becomes porous. (It would show as a matt white spot, if you could see it.) They usually occur between the teeth or at the bottom of the fissures. Even the dentist has to use X-rays to find early decay. At this stage the fine protein support structure of the surface crystals is still intact and the demineralization is **reversible**, that is the crystals can reform. If the tooth is carefully kept clean of plaque, and sugar consumption is reduced, **remineralization** of these areas can eventually occur by deposits of crystals from minerals dissolved in saliva. In other words there is a flow of minerals out from the tooth and a flow back in from the saliva. In remineralization the 'in flow' is greater than the 'out flow'.

It is important to note the surprising fact that very early caries can be controlled and reversed **without fillings** by plaque control and eating very little sugar. Experiments are in progress with special remineralizing mouth rinses, to be used at home, which add to the natural effect of the saliva minerals. Also, it is now certain that the presence of fluoride

17

next to the tooth surface, whether from drinking water, toothpaste or other sources, tips the balance at any time in favour of remineralization. Fluoride seems to be a catalyst for the repair of early decay.

I had better add, at this stage, that not all small white spots you may see on your children's teeth are caused by decay. When they occur on the open flat surfaces of the front teeth, away from the gums, they are more likely to be the result of some common childhood illness, which disturbed the cells making the enamel when the teeth were forming in the jaws. Other spots, white or brown, are caused by too much fluoride when the teeth are forming.

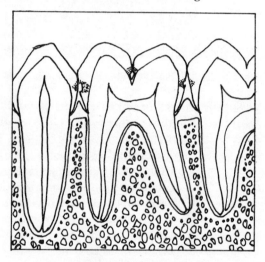

Fig. 3. Holes have appeared.

Returning to the story of decay, suppose that plaque is present and there is a lot of sugar in the diet, producing a lot of acid and dissolving a lot of the mineral crystals at some point on the tooth surface. Eventually, when enough of the crystals have been dissolved, the delicate protein framework will collapse. Once this has happened, complete remineralization is not possible and we have a **hole**.

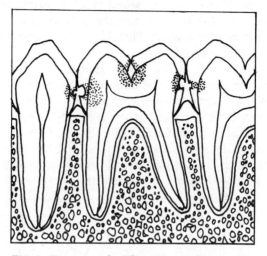

Fig. 4. Decay reaches dentine – pain may start.

It is very small at first, only just visible to the naked eye, but, as the bottom and sides of the hole are soon covered with plaque, the dissolving process goes on, and the hole gets bigger. After a while the hole reaches the end of the enamel. Even before this, the acid diffusing between the enamel crystals has started to dissolve the dentine underneath. Because dentine is softer (less crystalline), decay seems faster in dentine than in enamel, and the hole balloons out underneath.

Another change may happen at this stage – the tooth **may** begin to hurt. Enamel is completely insensitive, and enamel caries causes no pain at all. But the dentine has some fine nerve fibres, as well as thin tubes left by the cells which made the dentine, and both of these are sensitive to the acid which is produced by sugar getting into the plaque at the bottom of the hole. You may have noticed, if you had decay in a tooth, that sweet drinks or food made the tooth ache, although not everybody seems to suffer from toothache when caries strikes dentine. This is unfortunate, because

19

having toothache lets you know that something is going wrong in a tooth, and you can then go to a dentist to deal with it. Some of the worst decay occurs in people who have no pain, and think their teeth are fine. They may not get toothache until the final stage is reached.

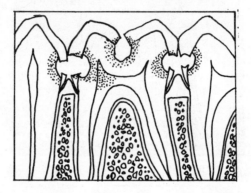

Fig. 5. Decay reaches pulp – pain probable.

The final stage is when the decay has passed right through the enamel and dentine and reached the nerve in the middle, or if you would like to use the proper term for it, **the pulp**. When the bacteria from the plaque reach the pulp, they infect it, and toothache starts in earnest. It changes from a sharp pain, or twinge brought on by sweet, hot, or cold things, to a continuous, sometimes throbbing, pain. It can be a very severe pain indeed preventing sleep, causing exhaustion, interfering with any possibility of work or mental concentration. It seems particularly cruel in young children, who have little responsibility for having caused it in the first place. Often the only thing a sufferer wants is to have the tooth taken out, even a front tooth, just to stop the pain. This is usually unnecessary, for there is a simple thing (which I shall mention in a minute) that a dentist can do to relieve the pain without removing the tooth.

The pain is caused by inflammation of the pulp with

resulting build-up of pressure. Since the tooth around the pulp is rigid and the hole at the end of a completely formed root very small, the inflamed tissue cannot expand. The pressure builds up fast causing the blood-vessels in the pulp to collapse, and the pain gets worse. If the pressure finally bursts through the hole at the end of the root (by which the nerves and blood-vessels enter the pulp), the pain may reduce, though the gum will probably swell up correspondingly as it becomes inflamed. The simple thing that the dentist can do is to drill a small hole through the tooth wall into the pulp and release the pressure. The pulp, already in the last stages of dying, will have to be removed at a later date and a filling put inside the tooth to block up the hole at the end of the root. This will prevent any bacteria entering. The tooth will have been saved and should last for years, often for a lifetime.

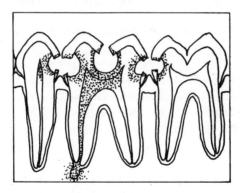

Fig. 6. Abscess forming at end of root.

TOOTH DECAY EQUATION

This somewhat dramatic sequence of events is extremely common, but I stress again that it is completely avoidable. A simple equation will help explain the requirements for decay, and by implication what can be done to prevent it.

$$\text{PLAQUE} + \text{SUGAR} \rightarrow \text{ACID}$$
$$\text{ACID} + \text{TOOTH} \rightarrow \text{DECAY}$$

If you cancel out any of these factors, you don't get decay. This is how it works:

1. Sugar

If you had absolutely no sugar in your diet, you would have no decay. This is exactly what we find in underdeveloped areas of the world where they don't have any sugar. In Britain, before the 1840s, when sugar was a luxury item only afforded by the very rich, decay occurred in less than 3 per cent of the population. Then sugar imported from the Caribbean became plentiful and cheap. The result was that within a few decades decay affected 90 per cent of the British population.

Nowadays in the industrial West it is difficult to avoid all sugar because so many manufactured foods have sugar added, but we can, with many advantages, cut down on the amount and especially the **frequency** with which we and our children have sugar in food.

2. Plaque

Theoretically, if you removed plaque completely from every tooth surface every two hours or so, you could eat a great deal of sugar without getting decay, because there would be nothing to turn sugar into acid. Two factors make this ideal impossible. First, it would be, for most of us, highly impractical to clean our teeth that often. And, second, even if we did, there are some areas of the teeth which are impossible to clean. These are natural crevices, called **fissures**, in the biting surfaces of the back teeth, which as they get deeper, become narrower than a single bristle of a tooth-brush. Beyond this point plaque remains permanently and cannot be removed, even by a dentist. There is, however, an answer to this, a kind of varnish called fissure sealant, which will be discussed later.

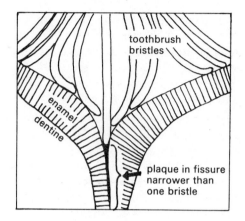

Fig. 7. Toothbrush not cleaning a fissure.

Although I have said that it is difficult to prevent decay by plaque removal alone or by sugar control alone, the **combination** of careful plaque removal every day and reduction in the amount and frequency of sugar, at and between meals, is **highly effective** in preventing decay. It often prevents even fissure decay.

3. Acid

What about removing the acid by neutralizing it with an alkali? This is not possible because the flow of saliva washes away any soluble substances put into the mouth, and also because the acid attack takes place under the plaque film, which would protect it from the alkali. It is for this second reason that simply rinsing the mouth with water after a meal will not remove the acid, though it may dilute it and the sugar in the outer layers of the plaque film. One experiment was tried by putting a small amount of urea into toothpaste. Certain plaque bacteria turn this into ammonia which neutralizes acid. But the results were not impressive.

4. Tooth

Removing the tooth is a highly effective way of stopping decay and unfortunately it is a very common method in most parts of the world. But the effects of tooth loss may be, in the long term, more serious and debilitating than the immediate effects of decay (see Chapter 11). Alternatively you can increase the tooth's resistance to decay with fluoride and fissure sealant (see Chapter 9).

5. Decay

So far we have considered the tooth decay equation to see whether it is possible to prevent decay by eliminating each factor. But, of course, decay itself can be removed, and, if it has not progressed a long way down the root, the undecayed part of the tooth can be saved. This is what a dentist does when he puts a filling in a tooth, and to some extent it is preventive too. It prevents further decay at that site if it is a good filling, and if the patient's sugar control is adequate. But a filling or an artificial crown, even a good one, is never a perfect fit. If you look at the junction of filling and tooth under the microscope, you will see a space between them, very small but still big enough for bacteria from plaque to get in. And sometimes, especially when sugar control is poor, new decay breaks out underneath a filling, and it has to be replaced. Each time a filling is replaced it gets bigger, and eventually the walls of the tooth get so weak that they break, usually when you are chewing. And this requires more complicated types of filling, and more visits to the dentist. So removing decay and filling the hole is not nearly so good as not having the decay in the first place.

Saliva flow

A number of illnesses and medical treatments cause the

flow of saliva to be reduced, and people suffering from the resulting dry mouth, or in technical language 'xerostomia' (pronounced zero-stome-ia), tend to have much more rapid decay than normal. This has focused attention on the important role which saliva plays in preserving the health of the teeth. First, a good saliva flow tends to wash out the mouth, including any sugar in it, and also to reduce the stickiness of potentially sticky foods. In other words it is a good dilutent and lubricant. Secondly, it has a 'buffering' effect, by which it tends to reduce the acidity in plaque caused by sugar. Thirdly, it contains antibodies and other antibacterial agents which control the growth of several decay-producing bacteria in the plaque. And finally, as we have seen, it contains dissolved minerals which can cause remineralization of early decay after acid attack. Small wonder that insufficient saliva is a powerful accelerator of tooth destruction.

Many of the conditions which cause xerostomia are fortunately rare, though it is worth knowing about them. Radiotherapy (e.g. X-ray treatment) to the head or neck for cancer treatment causes the saliva glands to dry up for months or years and this can result in spectacular decay rates, as can surgical removal of some of the saliva glands for a similar condition. Acute viral infection of the glands can produce temporary reduction in saliva.

There are, however, some more common complaints such as diabetes mellitus and Parkinson's disease which are associated with dry mouth. And a number of drugs, prescribed for conditions as diverse as stomach ulcers, anxiety/depression, insomnia, allergies, Parkinsonism, hypertension (high blood pressure), and appetite control, can cause xerostomia and thus be dangerous for the teeth if their use is prolonged beyond a few weeks. So if you or any members of your family (with natural teeth) are receiving prolonged treatment with antidepressants or tranquillizers (for anxiety, depression, or 'nerves'), antihistamines (for allergies, hay fever, or nausea), sedative-hypnotics (for insomnia), anticholinergics (for gastric ulcers or Parkinson's disease), adrenergic neurone blocking drugs – I do apologize for this pharmaceutical jargon – (for hypertension), or appetite suppressants, and you have noticed a dryness of the mouth after taking the drug, this might have dental consequences. The problem may be made worse by the high sugar content of some of the medicines. If your doctor is unwilling to alter the medication, or you are yourself, because it works, it is worth seeking dental advice.

The decay caused by xerostomia, of whatever cause, may be reduced or prevented at home by daily fluoride rinses, good oral hygiene (with fluoride toothpaste) and very careful control of sugar intake. Artificial saliva substitutes are available in some countries.

A final comment on this subject is that a dry mouth is quite normal during sleep, when the activity of the saliva glands is minimal. The reduced saliva flow allows bacterial products to accumulate in the plaque, and this accounts for the rather unpleasant smell and taste which many of us have in our mouths on waking. So cleaning the teeth is very important just before going to bed.

'WHAT ARE THE OTHER POSSIBILITIES FOR PREVENT-ING DECAY?'

By now some of these may have occurred to you, and to make the story complete I had better deal with them. However, most are of academic interest only, so you can omit this section quite safely and go straight to the summary.

What about – chemicals to kill bacteria that produce acid?
– making the surface crystals of the teeth more insoluble?
– covering the whole crown of the tooth with something to stop the acid getting to it?

- inoculating babies with harmless bacteria to stop the decay–producing ones from moving in, or vaccinating them against those bacteria?
- some substance which breaks down the glucan glue?

All these approaches have been tried, but few of them with complete success.

Chemicals to kill the plaque bacteria

Bacteria have the ability to adapt to most chemicals if they are used for more than a few days or weeks. For example, several kinds of bacteria can start to produce an enzyme which destroys penicillin, and these bacteria become penicillin resistant, so the drug will not work against them. Of course, there are limits in resistance to chemicals. I don't suppose that any bacterium could develop a resistance to concentrated nitric acid, but obviously you can't rinse your mouth with it.

One chemical which has been found to be effective against plaque is **chlorhexidine**. This is sold in chemist shops in Britain as Corsodyl Mouthwash, or in a jelly form, Corsodyl Gel, to be used like toothpaste. But some of the bacteria adapt to it after a few days, and, though the plaque is much reduced, it is not completely eliminated, which it would have to be to prevent all decay. There are two other disadvantages. First, it has a bitter taste which children would find unpleasant, and second, it forms a yellowish film on the teeth after being used for several weeks. This can be brushed off but with difficulty. Chlorhexidine is now widely applied for short periods to help plaque control after gum surgery, and for some mouth ulcers and infections, but it is not much used against decay. Chlorhexidine is not widely available in the United States, but some bactericidal effect may result from the fluoride mouth rinses which are used in North America.

Making the crystals in the tooth surface more insoluble

This has been really successful where it has been used. The effect is produced by fluoride (see Chapter 9).

Covering the tooth surface with something to stop the acid reaching it

Fissure sealants, varnishes which are attached to the tooth surface in the fissures, are also described in Chapter 9. They are effective if carefully applied. An artificial crown, covering most of the visible part of a tooth, will also form a barrier to decay. But if the sugar consumption remains high, decay is likely to break out next to the edge of the crown and make matters even worse.

Vaccinating against plaque bacteria

Research is in progress on this subject. The difficulty is that there are many different types of bacteria in plaque, and several variants of some types. So vaccines would need to be very complex and perhaps adapted to different individuals. Scientists are having similar problems in preparing a vaccine against the common cold, and for similar reasons. One hopes that in due course these problems may be solved. Most interest at the moment is being shown in a purified protein antigen derived from *Streptococcus mutans*, the bacterium most implicated in causing decay. This vaccine has successfully prevented decay in animals.

Inoculating babies with harmless bacteria to discourage the decay-producing ones

The difficulty with this approach is to do it early enough. A baby is inoculated with the mother's bacteria as it is born, and bacteria can be recovered from its mouth within minutes. It has been found to be very difficult to establish 'foreign' strains of bacteria against these initial ones. Of course, most babies don't have teeth through in the mouth when they are born, and therefore there are no hard surfaces for the plaque-producing bacteria to grow on, so there is a possibility that this approach might work, but it hasn't been successful so far.

Using a substance to break down the glucan glues

Enzymes which break down these glues, and help unstick the plaque have been tried in the past, but not very successfully, and the researchers became discouraged. A recent revival of interest in this subject has been caused by an enzyme called mutanase. But it is early days, and such enzymes are not available, or proven, for general use in preventing dental disease.

SUMMARY OF PLAQUE, SUGAR, AND TOOTH DECAY

1. Plaque is a mixture of bacteria, saliva proteins, bacterial glues, and water, which forms on any hard surface in the mouth.
2. Everyone has plaque forming all the time on their teeth.
3. Food is not needed for plaque to form, though sugars make it thicker and stickier.
4. **PLAQUE + SUGAR → ACID; ACID + TOOTH → DECAY**
5. The acids produced in plaque demineralize the tooth surface by dissolving the crystals in it.
6. At an early stage this demineralization can be reversed if plaque removal is efficient and sugar consumption low.
7. When a hole has appeared in the tooth surface, re-mineralization cannot reform the tooth completely, though with sugar control a small hole may never need to be filled.

8. When decay reaches the dentine, some sensitivity to sweet, hot, or cold foods may begin.

9. When the bacteria reach the pulp, it becomes infected and usually dies. The pain is worse because pressure builds up inside the tooth.

10. If the pressure bursts through the hole in the end of the root, the pain may lessen, but the gum around the root may swell up and discharge (a gumboil).

11. It is not necessary to remove teeth when these infections occur. Instead, the dead or dying pulp can be removed and the root, or roots, filled. This is a tricky job to do well, and requires several visits to the dentist. However, most dentists would prefer this treatment for themselves and their patients rather than losing teeth.

12. Not getting pain or sensitivity with decay is a disadvantage, because you may not know that anything is wrong.

To help fix these matters in your mind, here are some questions for you. You might like to check your answers with those on p.144.

1. It is better to clean your teeth before or after a meal?

2. Can you get decay from a meal which does not contain any foods with sugar in them?

3. Is it possible to eat sugary foods without getting decay?

4. Are yellowish teeth more or less resistant to decay than white teeth? (I didn't mention this – see if you can work it out.)

5. Why do teeth decay less as you get older?

5

Sugar

In the previous chapter I talked generally about the effect of sugar in producing decay, but without saying much about what kinds of sugar there are and what foods and drinks contain them.

First there is the sugar you buy **as** sugar to put into coffee or tea, make cakes, jam, and puddings with, add to cereals, and put into babies bottles (alas). At least you know where you are with this sugar because **you** are the person who adds it. But there are a multitude of prepared foods and drinks which you might be surprised to learn contain sugar. What about tomato ketchup, for example? Or packets of dried soup? Or canned spaghetti and baked beans? Or tins of peas? These all contain sugar, added to improve the flavour and to make it more acceptable to a society very much used to having sugar in things. Sometimes the ingredients are listed on the packaging – try browsing through the tins, bottles, and packets on your kitchen shelves to see which mention sugar. But not all products state their ingredients, so I am going to discuss the types of products and natural foods and drinks which contain sugar (also refer to information package 'C'). Medicines also often contain high concentrations of sugar, ironically, especially in children's syrups, and I shall relay what I can find out about these (see page 161). First, however, there are one or two questions of attitude and approach to sugar, and a little more of the technical side which you need to consider if you are to arrive at the best answers for your family.

SUGAR AND HEALTH

Sugar may be bad for the teeth, but it has a more sinister effect than this. It makes people ill by making them fat. Fatness, technically called obesity, is linked with high blood pressure, and high sugar intake with coronary heart disease and one kind of diabetes which appears in adults (late-onset diabetes). As you know, all these can be fatal.

Fat people obviously have other problems, too, social problems, like people who feel unattractive because they are overweight, or who get tired lugging around extra fat and not being able to do some of the things they used to do. I should not be surprised to learn that fat people are at a disadvantage in competing for jobs. All this makes sugar sound like a poison. In one sense it is a poison, though it is also a food. What decides whether it is a poison, is how much you have in relation to how much energy you use up. Most of us eat much more sugar than we can burn up for energy. Excess sugar is converted by the body into fat. It is particularly harmful to children. Fat babies are **unhealthy** babies!

A recent report on obesity by the Royal College of Physicians (England) has recommended that we reduce our sugar intake (about 38 kg per person per year in both the UK and USA) by half. Fifty per cent of this sugar intake is in the form of 'hidden sugar' in manufactured foods and drinks, and so the remainder – sugar used in the home for cooking, adding to breakfast cereals, tea, coffee, etc. – ought not to exceed one 1 kg packet per person every six weeks or so. For small children it should be less. If you are a family of four people including children, you probably should not be buying more than 1 kg of sugar for the entire family every fortnight. The typical British or American family buys about three times this amount of packet sugar, or 1.5 kg (over 3 lb) every week. And they receive the same again, or slightly more, in manufactured products.

Of course, sugar isn't really necessary in the diet at all. Millions of quite healthy people in the world don't have access to any sugar. The energy or calories they need to grow and stay alive are easily available from non-sugar carbohydrates, proteins and fats. But sugar is nice, mixed with other things, and because people like it, sugar is big business. In the UK in 1978 the money spent on confectionery was one and a half times the expenditure on bread, and that represented only a quarter of the sugar consumption.

In the more affluent parts of the world, health education is growing fast. People are becoming interested in how to stay healthy, as is shown by the increasing number of television programmes and newspaper features on health topics and the growing interest in exercise. People know it is bad to be fat, and not just because of appearance. The number of slimming magazines and organizations is increasing, and the annual consumption of sugar, especially table sugar, is starting to drop, so that sugar companies are having to do lots of research into alternative uses for sugar (fuel, plastics, etc.). But in one sector the effect is not so marked, that of confectionery and soft drinks for the children.

SUGAR IN CONFECTIONERY AND SOFT DRINKS

It is part of our culture to give sweets, sweet biscuits (or candies, lollies, and cookies as they are variously called), and chocolates to children. They tend to spend their pocket money on them. Sweets are a currency of affection or trading among school children. Even dentists fight pitched battles with their own parents to stop them giving confectionery to their grandchildren, it seems such a natural thing to do.

I was attending a slimming class once and the group was talking about the difficulty caused by having chocolates and sweets in the house for the children. The woman running the meeting said that this was a real problem, because it was clearly unfair to the children to banish sweets from the house just to make it easier for the mother or father to lose weight. When I asked why it was unfair, there was a slightly shocked silence, so deeply ingrained was the idea that sweets are a children's right. Yet at least 10 per cent of children in Britain are clinically obese, that is to say they weigh over 20 per cent more than their maximum healthy weight for their height, and they are likely to become among the 35 per cent of adults who are overweight. And some of them will die prematurely as a result. One very important reason for this is very high intake of sugar among our children.

Sensing the greater concern with health, some confectionery companies are advertising their products as if they were 'health foods'. Claiming that they are full of energy, which they are, it is suggested that you might be neglecting your children if you do not give them a this or that bar between meals to keep up their energy. Of course, it doesn't really make sense, if you think about it, that children, however active, are likely to starve between meals; but it is a clever way of counteracting vague doubts a mother may have about the healthiness of sweets, by reinforcing her anxieties as to whether she is looking after her children properly.

Sweets are also used to gain peace. If a child is crying or demanding attention in some other way and you need a few moments of quiet to concentrate on what you are doing, giving him something sweet to suck will probably work. At least it will stop the noise. Eventually this behaviour may be reinforced: a bored child may cry in order to get sweets, and a stressed mother may become conditioned to give them.

Dentists who specialize in treating children try to take some time in educating mothers about tooth decay. Most of the children's dentists I know have at least one story about how they had just finished explaining to a mother about sweets and decay, she nodding with understanding, when the toddler started to demand attention, or make a noise. Immediately the mother passed the child a chocolate bar or lollipop which she was carrying in her shopping bag for the purpose. Although the timing makes this rather funny, it is also understandable. We are not accustomed to thinking of children as powerful little manipulators of adults. But of course they are, and they have, quite naturally and properly, all sorts of ways of getting what they want. This is part of their survival behaviour. What you have to decide is whether you want them to become addicted to sugar by giving it to them as babies, or whether you are prepared to make a stand against the considerable demands for sweet things, once the taste for them has been established.

To answer 'no' to either of these questions requires courage and determination. You would have to become something of a pioneer in a much needed change in child-rearing practice. You would have to resist the tremendous inertial force of tradition; of what your mother told you, or aunts, or parents of your own age, even perhaps of what you have been told in hospitals or clinics. To go against this may seem a daunting prospect, especially if you happen to be expecting your first child. But consider what has been contained within 'tradition', the application of leeches to the weak child in Europe, the binding of feet in Chinese children, and more recently in many parts of the world the continuation of a purely liquid diet for a baby over several months old and the almost complete rejection of breast-feeding. Nowadays such traditions seem stupid, but perhaps an earlier one, of choosing savoury foods, is worth recapturing.

If you need further motivation, consider yourself. Do you have trouble resisting sweet things? Are you overweight? Have you lost any teeth through decay? Do you have lots of fillings? If the answer is 'yes' to any of these questions, you may wish to make it 'no' for your children.

SUGAR AND BABIES

While there is no absolute proof, there is much circumstantial evidence that a taste for sweet things is established very early in a child's life. This 'sweet tooth' is maintained and encouraged by adding sugar to babies' bottles, or giving them sweetened fruit drinks and desserts. 'If he won't take the bottle, try adding a little sugar'. Mothers have told me that once they had done this, the child would not accept unsweetened milk, for example. Adding sugar to babies' food is a very bad idea, and not only for the teeth. Putting sweet things on dummies is also bad, as is putting a baby to sleep with a bottle of milk or fruit juice. If a bottle is necessary as a pacifier during the night (I don't mean for specific timed or demand feeding) it should contain plain water.

An interesting recent study[1] showed that when mothers gave babies sweetened water to drink (water plus table sugar, honey, or syrup) during the first six months of life, the babies showed a significant preference for sugar solution over plain water. The experiment was carried out as follows. A day or so after birth about 200 babies, whose parents had agreed to take part, were offered bottles with specially accurate nipples containing plain water, then weak sugar solution, then stronger sugar solution, then the same drinks in reverse order, for one minute each time with resting periods in between. The quantities drunk were measured. Typically, the new-born babies drank three times as much sweetened water as plain water. Six months later the experiment was repeated, only this time the parents completed a seven-day diet diary for their children. Those babies who had been given sweetened drinks during the first six months still showed a three-to-one preference for the sugar solutions. But those babies who had been given plain water to drink, while they also drank more of the sugar solutions than plain water at the six months test, their preference for sugar solutions measured by consumption was exactly half that of the 'sugar babies'. In other words they were losing, rather than maintaining, a taste for sweet things.

[1]Beauchamp, G.K. & Moran, M. Dietary experience & sweet taste preference in human infants. Appetite: *Journal for Intake Research* Vol. 3: pp.139–152 (1982).

It is not always easy to avoid sugar in prepared baby foods. You must look at the labels for contents, but even these may be misleading. I saw, for example, babies' blackcurrant and rose-hip syrup drinks, which proudly announced that they were sucrose-free. On examining the list of contents, I saw that glucose syrup had been used instead, which is scarcely better.

Even infants' liquid medicines are often marketed in a sugar syrup, and it is worth asking your doctor if he could prescribe a sugar-free syrup, especially if the medicine is to be taken for more than a few days (see p.161).

Baby rusks are another awful example. Until recently the typical sugar content of a manufactured rusk was 30 per cent by weight. Under pressure from dieticians and paediatricians, new versions, called low-sugar rusks have appeared in addition to the originals. But 'low-sugar' here means 15 to 18 per cent of the weight, so that each rusk still contains about a teaspoon of sugar – not a very edifying start for the teeth as they begin to appear in the mouth. As an alternative it is very simple to cut pieces of wholemeal bread to a handy size and bake them in the oven to make them crisp and strong.

(Note: Modern dietary advice is to avoid wheat flour products, including bread, cakes, and even home made rusks, until the age of six months. Rice flour, potato flour, and many others may be used instead. This very much reduces the chances of your child's developing an allergy to gluten, called coeliac disease, later in life. Gluten is a major protein in many varieties of wheat.)

SUGAR AT SCHOOL

At school there are further problems, because sweets are sometimes a status symbol and sometimes a way of gaining friends or expressing affection between children. It is very difficult to insist that your children do not do what other children do, because children hate to be different. Indeed, if you are too authoritarian about it, eating sweets may become an attractively forbidden activity like smoking, and done in secret. There is no easy answer to this difficulty. To make any impact on the school confectionery and soft drinks problem, you probably have to get the support of the teachers and some other parents at a PTA meeting (teachers are usually in favour of reducing sweet-eating). You can then suggest that the school tuck shop stocks alternatives to sweets, such as savoury snacks, sugar-free (diet) soft drinks, sugar-free chewing gum, nuts, and fruits. Some fruits are very attractive alternatives, such as peaches, when in season, and these are about half the cost of the smallest bar of chocolate.

At home, rather than forbidding sweets altogether, some dentists give their children sweets one day a week, say on Saturday after the midday meal, on the understanding that they will eat them all and not hoard some for another time. The children of dentists eventually become rather proud of not eating sweets, but their parents are highly motivated, and are able to explain the reasons well. On the other hand, if I am making this book as clear as I should like, then you should be in a very similar position.

SNACKS

A change in the eating patterns of children is taking place in Britain, the USA, and many other countries in the West. As more mothers are going out to work, for economic reasons as well as for interest, the classic three meals a day are being replaced, in part, by snacks which children or their parents buy to save time. It is doubtful that the 'little and often' idea of nutrition has advantages for general health – it may become a lot and too often – and many of the snacks have too much salt and fat as well as little dietary fibre. But many snack foods and drinks contain a great deal of sugar besides and, when taken often, provide the worst possible situation for teeth. (See the next section on sugar frequency.)

In order to tackle this problem the Health Education Council Dental Health Study at the University of Cambridge has been running a programme of teaching and motivating groups of children under five to choose safe (savoury) rather than unsafe (sweet) snacks. The 'Good Teeth Programme' lasts six weeks, involves the active participation of the parents, and also introduces the colouring of plaque with food dyes and its removal with a toothbrush.

The results of this study are encouraging. Six months later about two-thirds of the children, including some very young ones, are still able to choose safe rather than unsafe snacks. This shows that it is possible to encourage in young children safe behavioural patterns with food as with other things like crossing the road, and avoiding fire. This is an important confirmation of something not really very surprising: a mother or father can teach the choice of savoury rather than sweet. Furthermore, **children do like savoury food**. As we have seen, they persist in their taste for sweet things only when sweet things are repeatedly given to them. Why does this happen?

Here are some of the reasons. Health visitors and post-natal clinics may recommend vitamins in sugar-based syrups, or the addition of sugar to bottle feeds. Doctors may say, and may allow themselves to be quoted as saying, that children need sugar for energy, without pointing out at the same time that all of us make that necessary sugar in our bodies from everyday non-sugary foods (the Dental Health Study has coined the useful terms 'ready-made' versus 'body-made' sugars). It may not occur to mothers that plain water is better than fruit squash when a child is thirsty.

It is my belief that the greatest advocates of sweet snacks for children today (apart from the manufacturers) are grandparents and other relatives of that generation. Today's grandparents were children or teenagers during the Second World War when confectionery was difficult to get or unobtainable. It acquired a kind of glamour which persists.

Nowadays, sweets, chocolates, etc., are plentiful and cheap compared with other presents. And grandparents, not always well-off, want to show their love and affection by making these sweet gestures, which are usually well received. Grandparents regard eating sweets as a normal and desirable part of childhood. So the pressures and opportunities to have sweet snacks are many. But it is well worth resisting them.

The fact that 'snacking' is an increasingly important element in industrialized communities, has led to the manufacture in the United States of snack foods which are advertised as 'healthier'. Healthier in this sense means not only safe for the teeth, but also for general health. Low salt, low fat, and high fibre content are implied, as well as minimal or absent sugar. Talks are in progress in the UK between health experts and large food-retailing chains towards the marketing of similar snack foods.

PREGNANCY AND DENTAL DISEASE

There is a widespread belief that decay increases during pregnancy. 'A tooth for every child' is a phrase I have heard from several patients. This belief may appear to gain support from the fact that in some countries with public dental services dental care is provided free to pregnant and nursing mothers. The facts about decay are otherwise. There is no evidence that pregnancy has any effect on the rate of decay. It may be that a few pregnant women have developed a craving for specific sugary foods – say, maple walnut ice-cream, or chocolate bars, or honey – and have done their teeth some extra damage, but not enough in that short time to make a significant difference to the rate of extraction. The truth was more a matter of coincidence. By the time when most young women were having babies, the decay caused by childhood sugar-eating habits carried on into adolescence had reached a point where only heroic efforts could save the teeth, and some had passed that point.

Mothers concluded that it was pregnancy itself which was responsible, perhaps believing that the unborn baby was removing calcium from their teeth. That, too, is untrue. There is no way that calcium can be removed from the permanent tooth except by acid attack, wear, breakage, or the dentist's drill. Indeed, it seems that teeth have a high priority on any calcium available. A child, for example, would develop rickets before any of his teeth suffered through lack of calcium. In other words neither mother nor child suffer any disadvantage to the teeth themselves as a result of pregnancy.

What does happen, however, is that a pregnant woman's gums may suffer temporarily. There is a condition called 'pregnancy gingivitis' in which the gums are more susceptible to the effects of plaque. During pregnancy, hormonal changes prepare the body for childbirth and one effect is softening of the connective tissue, which holds the bones together, to allow the pelvis to expand during the birth. This connective tissue holds the healthy gums in shape – the fine 'orange peel' stippling of the healthy gum surface is the result of tiny connective tissue filaments holding it to the underlying bone – and when they are softened by hormonal changes, the gums may be more inclined to become inflamed and to bleed when plaque is imperfectly removed. Scrupulous brushing and flossing should prevent this. It is the same connective tissue which holds the teeth in their sockets, and I have known several pregnant women with healthy mouths who reported that they felt their teeth becoming slightly loose. The explanation above provided the necessary reassurance, and their teeth, along with any inflammation of the gums, returned to normal after pregnancy.

SUGAR FREQUENCY [THIS IS AN ESPECIALLY IMPORTANT SECTION]

In order to understand exactly what effect eating habits have on tooth decay, it is necessary to return (yet again) to the plaque on the tooth surface. You will remember that when sugar in solution diffuses into the plaque film, acid is produced by the bacteria. Also that, without that acid, the solubility of the calcium crystals in the tooth is so low that the tooth cannot dissolve them – or to be exact the minute traces of calcium salts going into solution in the saliva are balanced by those coming out of the saliva and being deposited back in the tooth. When acid is present this balance is upset, and more salts come out than go back in. But it takes a certain **minimum amount** of acid to upset the balance.

Acidity is measured in units called pH (pronounced as the letters of the alphabet). The pH scale runs from 14 to 0 in reverse, so that the lower the pH number the more acid the solution. Conversely, the higher the number the more alkaline the solution. At pH 7 there is no acidity or alkalinity in the solution and it is said to be neutral. Absolutely pure water is pH 7. Saliva is normally slightly acid, about pH 6.5 (though this changes a little with the rate of flow and at different times of day), and plaque is about the same.

Acid must accumulate in the plaque, and its pH fall below 5.7 at the tooth surface, before the balance is upset and the crystals start to dissolve. **pH 5.7 is called the critical pH for decay**.

What happens to the pH of plaque when you or your child starts to suck a sweet? There is predictable sequence of events:

1. Sugar dissolves in saliva pH 6.5.
2. Sugar solution diffuses into plaque film pH 6.5.
3. Immediate acid production – pH starts to fall.
4. One and a half minutes later pH passes critical 5.7, going down.
5. Tooth starts to decay.
6. Sweet sucking continues, pH continues to fall, tooth dissolves faster, bacteria multiply and make glucan glue.

7. Sweet finished, sugar in saliva gets swallowed but bacteria continue to work on sugar already in plaque, and start to produce acid from glucan glue. pH continues to fall, tooth dissolves faster.
8. After 6 minutes most of the plaque sugar is used up, pH starts to rise.
9. After 13 minutes pH rises above critical level, decay stops. (This is very variable, and can take longer. 13 minutes would be a minimum.)
10. After 25 minutes or longer, plaque pH is similar to that of saliva.

Conclusion

One sweet has produced about 12 minutes of decay. Any form of sugar will do, but the more concentrated the sugar (up to a point) the more acid is produced.

Now, that sequence of events took me 140 words to explain. It's much clearer with only 20 words and a graph. (If you want to blind your dentist with science this is called a **Stephan curve**, after the man who described it).

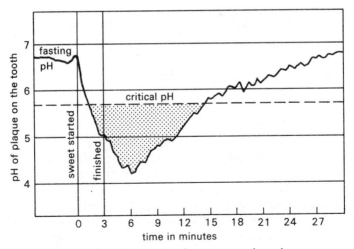

Fig. 8. Acid production in plaque on tooth surface.

Good mouthkeeping

The shaded area below the critical pH represents the amount of decay. Imagine that ten minutes after finishing the first sweet, your child starts another. The pH has not yet climbed into the safe area, when suddenly more sugar arrives, more acid is produced, down goes the pH, out come more minerals from the tooth. And so on.

If you are aged 25 or over, the same sort of decay can happen to you, though at a slower rate because your teeth have become more resistant. Dentists expect the decay rate of adults to fall considerably, if they have had the necessary fillings to deal with the damage already done. Occasionally we see adults who are getting a lot of new decay. Asking in detail about their diet invariably shows that they have sugar in some form many times a day. Usually they take sugar in tea or coffee, and drink a lot of it. Or they 'chain-suck' peppermints, or some other confectionery.

Imagine what similar habits will do to the more vulnerable teeth of children.

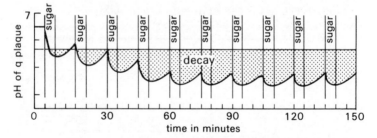

Fig. 9. Acid production with repeated exposure to sugar.

This shows the effect of sucking four sweets an hour at regular intervals. The decay is continuous and fast. In the two and a half hours shown here, less than one packet of mints will have been consumed.

It doesn't have to be sweets. It could be sips from cups of coffee or tea with sugar in them, or soft drinks, or sugar lumps, or pieces of chocolate, or any combination of these plus others.

44

Schoolchildren buy a lot of peppermints because they like them and because they are cheap. When I see schoolchildren with bad decay, we go through a diet analysis together, taking a typical day, from getting up in the morning to going to bed at night. They sometimes forget to mention peppermints because they have almost become part of the background of school life. I no longer ask them, 'How many peppermints do you have a day?' I ask them, 'How many packets of peppermints do you have a day – one, two, or more?' They often say one, two, two and a half even. Now each packet of the most popular brand contains 14 peppermints. Two packets a day represents 28 exposures to sugar from that source alone. It doesn't include sugar in soft drinks, at meal times, in bed-time snacks and so on. So some school children, and some adults for that matter, have their plaque below the critical pH for hours on end. The results are exactly what you would expect: massive tooth decay. Recently in England one peppermint manufacturer ran an advertising campaign with a picture of the product with slogans like, 'Don't forget to put holes in their stockings.' and, 'It's cool to have holes in your pockets.' Many dentists were rather shocked by this wording which strongly suggested to them that the last word in each case ought to read 'teeth'. Remember, peppermints are not worse for the teeth than other sugary sucking sweets, but they are very cheap, handily packaged, and widely available. In other words, the companies which market them are very good at their jobs. And the sweets certainly give pleasure.

What can be done about this? Well some changes are happening. In Britain at the moment there are two varieties of sugar-free chewing gum, Orbit and Trident, which will not harm the teeth. They contain non-sugar sweeteners called sorbitol and xylitol which are more expensive than sugar and so these brands are more expensive, though not a lot more. But you can, with a quiet mind, provide them for your children. In some other countries, where public health awareness is more advanced than in Britain, the sweet manufacturers are responding to pressure and making more sugar-free confectionery. In Switzerland a law has been passed which allows confectionery manufacturers, if they can prove that plaque pH does not fall below 5.7 with their products, to state on the packet that they are 'safe for teeth'. To achieve this the sweets would have to be sugar-free. To date, the sales of sugar-substituted chewing gums account for 50 per cent of the market in Switzerland and 70 per cent in Sweden. In the United States there are at least 9 different sucking candies which are sugar-free, and 19 sugar-free gums. Many countries, including Britain, have sugar-free soft drinks primarily intended for dieting. But only if they contain no sugar are they safe for teeth.

SUGAR QUANTITY

It used to be thought by dentists that it was only the frequency of sugar in the mouth which was important, not the total quantity at any one time. This idea is now losing favour because high concentrations of sugar encourage the sugar-using bacteria to multiply and to make more of the glucan glues, so more and thicker plaque is formed. Having a lot of sugar at once is therefore bad for teeth too, though not as bad as having it often. For the rest of the body the reverse is true – a large amount of sugar at one time is converted to more fat than the same amount spread out. However, reducing the frequency of sugary snacks is also likely to reduce the total amount of sugar catcn.

SUGAR CONTENT OF FOODS AND DRINKS

So that you know what types of food and drink are decay-producing and what are safe, I have prepared a list of the sugar contents of foods in the Information Package part C, see p.150.

SUMMARY ON SUGAR

1. Every time sugar reaches plaque on teeth, acid is produced.
2. Acidity is measured in pH; neutral is pH 7, acidity is less than pH 7. Saliva and plaque are about pH 6.5.
3. Critical pH for tooth decay is 5.7, and this is reached and passed within 2 minutes after the sugar reaches the plaque.
4. When the sugar in food and drink has been swallowed, it takes at least 13 minutes for the pH to rise above the critical level and tooth decay to stop.
5. Repeated exposure to sugar, as in 'chain-sucking' sweets (candies), and drinking lots of tea, coffee, or soft drinks containing sugar, keeps the pH below 5.7, resulting in continuous decay.
6. All this requires the presence of plaque, and will not happen immediately after all the plaque has been removed. But plaque reforms within a few hours.
7. The quantity of sugar eaten at one time affects the quantity of plaque produced, and general health; the frequency with which sugar is eaten affects the total time during which decay is going on.
8. In communities where there is no sugar in the diet, there is no decay.
9. In countries where the sugar consumption is increasing, the decay rate is also increasing. The converse is also true.
10. There is evidence that a taste for sweet things is maintained in babies by the addition of sugar to baby foods, milk and other drinks.
11. Not only does indulging a 'sweet tooth' cause decay, pain, visits to the dentist, and tooth loss, but it also causes fatness, arterial disease and heart failure, late-onset diabetes, and contributes to other diseases. Excess sugar is converted to fat which may be deposited on the walls of the arteries.

12. Children must be educated not to have sweets except on infrequent special occasions. Parents, grandparents, and other relatives and well-wishers must be educated not to give children sweets. They can give fruit, nuts, and other things instead.

13. Pressure must be put on schools to discourage the sale of sweets and consumption by children during school hours. 'Tuck shops' should be encouraged to stock fruit and savoury snacks which children can buy instead of sweets. 'Diet', or very-low-calorie drinks should be available in preference to conventional ones.

14. When doctors and other medical authorities say that sugar is necessary for energy, they are correct. But they are also irresponsible if they do not add that we make sugar more safely in our bodies from the sugarless food we eat. It is not necessary for health that a single sugar molecule passes anyone's lips.

15. Sugar control is more important for preventing tooth decay than any other measure. The children of dentists and dietitians tend to have no decay at all. The same will be true of any family which understands and acts on this summary.

More questions to test your understanding (Answers on p.146)

1. Why is it better for children to have sweets at meal times than between meals?

2. If a meal contains sugar anyway, does it make any difference to have sweets as well at the end of a meal?

3. Are natural foods containing sugar, such as honey, less decay-producing than manufactured foods to which sugar has been added?

4. Place the following foods in increasing order of decay production and then see if you are right by checking the list of sugar contents of foods pages 154–161: cheddar cheese, cola drinks, drinks with less than one calorie per can/bottle, boiled sweets (hard candy), apples, bread and butter, bread and jam, rose-hip syrup.

6

Types of sugar and alternative sweeteners

Since the first edition of this book four years ago, there have been many developments in the area of food sweeteners, sugars and 'non-sugar sweeteners'. And though the first edition of this book was written for parents with no specialized dental knowledge, experience has shown that it is widely referred to by people professionally engaged in dental and general health care. For these two reasons I have expanded the section on types of sugars and sweeteners considerably so that the interested reader may be brought up to date. The result may be too technical or detailed for some people, and to them I recommend a cursory glance. You may, however, want to read the sections 'Is glucose good for you (refer p.55) and the 'Caution on labelling' (refer p.67) in more detail. The sweetening compounds covered are listed below, with their alternative names.

NUTRITIVE SWEETENERS

Sugars (saccharides)

sucrose (cane sugar, beet sugar)
glucose (D-glucose, dextrose, grape sugar)
fructose (D-fructose, laevulose, fruit sugar)
lactose (lactobiose, milk sugar)
honey
maple syrup
glucose syrups (corn syrups, corn sweeteners)
high-fructose corn syrups (HFCS or high-fructose sweeteners)
invert sugar
hydrogenated glucose syrups (Lycasins®)
coupling sugars

Sugar alcohols (polyols, polyhydric alcohols)

sorbitol (D-glucitol, E420)
mannitol (manna sugar, E421)
xylitol
isomalt (Palatinit®)

NON-NUTRITIVE SWEETENERS (INTENSE SWEETENERS)

aspartame (L-aspartyl-L-phenylalanine methyl ester, Canderel®)
acesulfame-K (acesulfame potassium)
saccharine (sodium saccharine, calcium saccharine)
thaumatin (Talin®)
cyclamate (sodium or calcium cyclohexylsulphamate)
stevioside
glycyrrhizin (ammoniated glycyrrhizin)
neohesperidin dihydrochalcone (neo-DHC)
trichlorogalactosucrose (TGS)
miraculin
monellin
cynarin

SUGARS

Sucrose

What we commonly call sugar (cane or beet sugar) is actually sucrose. A variety of chemically related compounds exist and all of them are sugars. Sucrose is a compound of two other sugars, glucose and fructose, and is rapidly broken down to these in the gut before being absorbed into the body. It is available in a variety of forms, either white or brown.

White sugar is sold as granulated, caster, icing, and preserving sugar, and as sugar lumps and 'coffee crystals'.

Brown sugar is sold as raw cane sugar (also called muscovado, Barbados, and molasses sugar), Demerara, and soft brown sugar. The different shades of brown are due to incomplete removal, or subsequent addition, of molasses (molasses and black treacle are residues left during the refining of sugar).

All variants of white and brown sugar are almost 100 per cent sucrose.

Sucrose is thought to be **worse** for the teeth than other sugars because it forms more of the glucan glues, and makes the plaque thicker and stickier. It is also unfortunately the most abundant sugar, and the most used by the food manufacturers all over the world as a food additive.

Glucose (D–glucose, dextrose, grape sugar)

This sugar, which occurs widely in nature, is also added to some foods and drinks, especially in the United States where glucose syrups (see below) made from corn (maize) starch are becoming cheaper than sucrose. Glucose is not as sweet as sucrose (about 70 per cent) but it is used to bring out the fruit flavour of soft drinks and jams. Some people believe that glucose, in, for example, the form of proprietary 'healing' drinks, is the ideal form of energy food. The arguments against this notion are presented below in the section called 'Is glucose good for you?' (see p.55). Glucose is certainly **bad for the teeth**.

Fructose (D–fructose, laevulose, fruit sugar)

This sugar is found in certain fruits and vegetables, and in honey. It is 1.7 times as sweet as sucrose, and is also said to improve the flavour of jams, fruit drinks, sorbets, etc., but in a pure form it is more expensive than sucrose or glucose. In high fructose corn syrups (see below) the problem of cost has been overcome.

Fructose is easily broken down to acids by plaque bacteria and so it is bad for teeth when added as a sweetener. This also applies to honey, but the concentrations in fresh fruit are fairly low, the pieces of fruit are usually swallowed quickly, and the stimulation of saliva flow is beneficial to the teeth.

51

Interesting evidence on the role of sugars in causing tooth decay comes from the study of children suffering from a rare genetic disorder called hereditary fructose intolerance (HFI). The symptoms are first noticed at weaning when infants start to receive food containing sucrose or fructose (remember sucrose is a compound of glucose and fructose). These babies develop alarming symptoms of sweating, vomiting, tremors, and even coma and convulsions. If they continue to receive these sugars, they fail to thrive and develop jaundice, large livers, and a variety of other metabolic disturbances. If HFI is diagnosed, and they survive, these children learn to avoid all desserts, cakes, confectionery, and most fruits. But they can eat unsweetened milk products, glucose, and starch products like bread, rice, potatoes, oats, etc. It has been noticed since 1956, when the disease was first identified, that the teeth of people with HFI are much better than those of the general population. About half of them have no decay at all, and those that do have only about 10 per cent of the decay experienced by people of the same age with normal fructose metabolism. Also the plaque of HFI sufferers contains much lower numbers of acid-producing bacteria. This evidence supports the view that starchy foods do not produce decay, and that low sugar intake alters dental plaque in a beneficial way.

Lactose (lactobiose, milk sugar)

This sugar, found only in milk, is a compound of two simpler sugars, glucose and galactose. It has a low solubility in water and low sweetness (one-sixth that of sucrose) which limits its suitability as a food additive. Lactose is not particularly good for the teeth, but it is consumed in low concentrations (4.7 per cent in cow's milk, 6.9 per cent in human milk) and is normally not implicated in tooth decay. However bottle or breast feeding, when prolonged or very frequent, can produce decay, typically found on the back surfaces of the upper front teeth ('bottle caries').

Honey

This is mainly composed of glucose and fructose. There is a belief that because it is a naturally made product which has not been manufactured it is somehow better for you than other sugar sources. In fact sugar and water make up 99.4 per cent of honey, and the remaining 0.6 per cent contains little of any food value except minute traces of a few vitamins. It is a very expensive energy source, but has more interesting flavours than refined sugars. It is as **bad for the teeth** as any other sugar of the same high concentration except sucrose, and it is nearly as bad as sucrose.

Maple syrup

Made from the sap of a type of maple tree, it is mainly sucrose and water. **Bad for the teeth**.

Since the 1960s there has been rapid growth in the manufacture of sugary syrups, known generally as 'starch hydrolysates', which are produced industrially from the starches in cereals and potatoes. It is worth knowing about these because they are increasingly found on food labels.

Glucose syrups (corn syrups, corn sweeteners)

These are produced by treating starches with acids or enzymes under controlled conditions, whereupon they break down to mixtures of glucose, maltose, and more complex sugars. By varying the conditions it is possible to produce syrups tailor-made for different food and drink applications. The low price of corn starch has made these sugars so competitive that the European Economic Community has imposed economic controls to protect the sugar growers. Nevertheless, their use is increasing on both sides of the Atlantic. Not much research has been done on the dental implications of these sweeteners, but from their composition it is expected that they will turn out to be **only slightly better than sucrose**. So if you see a food or drink labelled 'sucrose free', check the label carefully to see if it mentions glucose or any other syrups.

High fructose corn syrups (HFCS or high-fructose syrups)

These are modifications of glucose syrups in which an enzyme is used to convert some of the glucose to fructose. A typical composition is 50 per cent glucose, 42 per cent fructose and 8 per cent more complex sugars. The point of this is that the greater sweetness of fructose compensates for the reduced sweetness of glucose and produces a mixture with about the same sweetness as sucrose, while being cheaper. They are mainly used in soft drinks at present (e.g. colas in the USA), but their general use in the food industry is rising rapidly. The decay-producing properties of HFCS are likely to be similar to those of the glucose syrups, that is **only slightly better than sucrose.**

Invert sugar

This is syrup produced by hydrolysis of sucrose solution, which produces a mixture of glucose and fructose and is sometimes added to foodstuffs. Its constitution is like that of honey and therefore **bad for the teeth**.

Hydrogenated glucose syrups (Lycasins®)

These are also produced from glucose syrups in which some of the glucose is converted to sorbitol (see below). They were generally developed (from 1960) in order to produce a 'boiled sweet' (hard candy) without sucrose and with a reduced tendency to generate acid in dental plaque. To date, studies suggest that Lycasins are **significantly less decay-producing than sucrose** in confectionery, and a number of products based on Lycasins have been approved as 'safe for teeth' in

Switzerland. They have recently been licensed in the UK.

Coupling sugars

So far used only in Japan, these are products made by reacting starch and sucrose together with an enzyme. The result is a mixture of sucrose molecules with varying numbers of glucose molecules tacked on. This sounds fairly deadly for the teeth, but in fact the extra complexity of these sugar molecules appears to make it more difficult for plaque bacteria to produce acid or glucan glues. Various foods are sweetened with coupling sugars in Japan (they are about half as sweet as sucrose), and tests have shown that they are **much less decay-producing than sucrose.**

IS GLUCOSE GOOD FOR YOU?

The idea that sugar, especially glucose, is a super-fast energy source is quite true, and quite irrelevant. Even marathon runners, who make tremendous energy demands on their bodies, prefer to build up their energy stores before the race with starchy foods instead of popping glucose tablets during the race. The drinks they get along the way are mainly to replenish water and salt loss. The few grams of sugar in these drinks are there not as a major energy source, but to prevent acidosis from the metabolism of body fats during the race. Worse than irrelevant, fast sugar can be harmful.

What happens to sugars in the body

When sucrose is eaten, it is first broken down to its component molecules, glucose and fructose, by an enzyme in the cells lining the small intestine. Glucose is then rapidly absorbed and passed to the bloodstream by an active 'transport system', and fructose by a slower process. On reaching the blood, glucose stimulates the production of insulin from special cells in the pancreas. Insulin has several functions, but in this context it does two things. It allows glucose to pass into muscle and fat cells, and it also stimulates the production of an enzyme which converts glucose into a more active form, either for energy production, or, more often, for storage in the liver. Both of these actions effectively remove glucose from the blood. (Fructose metabolism is initially independent of insulin but can later join the same pathways.) The activity of insulin in lowering blood glucose levels is balanced by another hormone, glucagon, which has the opposite effect. In particular, it causes the storage form of glucose, known as glycogen, to be converted back to glucose and released from the liver into the circulating blood. All these changes can happen very fast, on demand, and constitute a beautifully tuned mechanism which keeps the blood sugar (glucose) between certain limits.

What happens when fast sugar, a large dose of sucrose or glucose, suddenly arrives in the intestine? Many people appear to handle it without difficulty, but the initial surge in the blood glucose level produces a large insulin release which causes a drop in the glucose level to below normal about an hour later. This over-secretion of insulin may make you feel hungry even though you have had more 'calories' than you need. Meantime some of the glucose is being converted into fat in the fat cells.

With a large dose of glucose, some people tend to produce a lot of insulin, which causes their blood sugar concentration to drop like a stone and a condition occurs called, in medical jargon, hypoglycaemia (pronounced high-po-gly-**seem**ier). This produces feelings of weakness, trembling, hunger, headache, and irritability. Indeed, hypoglycaemia may be a factor in the lives of some business men who have only 'liquid lunches' consisting of gins and tonic. Initially the alcohol and the sugar in the tonic water produce a feeling of well-being. But by mid-afternoon the business man, now back in his office, may be starting to feel a bit wobbly. The effective answer to this may seem to be another drink. And so on. Many people who have the symptoms of hypoglycaemia following intake of sugar have found that eating more complex carbohydrates instead, like bread, potatoes, rice, etc., solves the problem, because the glucose needed for energy is produced from unsweetened starchy foods at a gentle, controlled rate. This is because there are extra steps required to break the complex starch molecules down to the simple sugars from which they have originally formed in the potato plant. Starch is, in effect, slow-release sugar. There is no overshoot in insulin production.

This slow release of glucose is also important for people who can produce no insulin or only small amounts, the diabetics, because their control of the blood glucose levels is even more precarious.

It may seem to you that in advocating starchy foods, like bread and potatoes, I am breaking all the rules of slimming and weight control. But modern ideas of nutrition are undergoing a revolution and it is now believed that complex carbohydrates, with the dietary fibre still in them, are not fattening. Bread with a high bran content, potatoes in their skins, brown rice, beans, and the like have a capacity to make you feel 'full up'. The real culprits now seem to be fats (e.g. the dollops of butter put on the bread and potatoes) and sugars, which can make you feel hungry soon after eating. Any glucose superfluous to energy requirements is very readily converted to fats.

One final observation on the advisability of starches rather than sugars as the source of carbohydrate food. All the delicately controlled energy-regulating systems of the human body, of which I have mentioned only two, have taken millions of years of evolutionary trial and error to perfect. During most of that time starches were the staple diet and sugar was available only in the low concentrations which occur naturally in fruits and vegetables, with perhaps the occasional taste of honey. Only during the last hundred and fifty years has sugar been available in a refined concentrated form and in quantity. It is hardly to be expected that the human metabolism could, in so short a time, have transformed itself to cope successfully with the 110 g (4 oz.) average daily sucrose intake of people in the affluent or sugar-producing parts of the world.

Non-sugar sweeteners

In order to bypass the diseases caused by high sugar consumption, and to meet the increasing demand for low calorie foods and drinks in industrialized countries where the taste for sweet things is endemic, much effort is being put into developing alternatives which taste like sucrose and are safer. The results of this research and development may be divided into two categories of non-sugar sweeteners: those which have calorific value (nutritive sweeteners) and those which do not (non-nutritive sweeteners).

NUTRITIVE SWEETENERS

These include the sugar alcohols, of which the most promising are sorbitol, mannitol and xylitol, plus a relatively new proprietary combination of sugar alcohols called Palatinit® or isomalt. (Don't be alarmed, or excited, by the word 'alcohol' in this context – sugar alcohols are relatively large molecules and not in the least intoxicating).

Sorbitol (D-glucitol)

This is a sugar alcohol, or polyol, which occurs naturally in some ripe fruit (cherries, plums, pears, and apples), but which is produced commercially from sucrose or starch. It has about half the sweetness of sucrose. It is slowly and incompletely absorbed from the gut, and subsequent metabolic changes are also slow, so that it has been widely used as a sucrose substitute in diabetic preparations. However, the calorific value of these foods is as high as conventionally sweetened food, which is a disadvantage for diabetics trying to control their weight, and there is some uncertainty as to whether it is absolutely safe for teeth. Initially, plaque bacteria fail to convert it to acids, but it seems likely that with repeated exposure to sorbitol they would adapt and start using it. None the less, at the moment it is regarded as **much less cariogenic (decay-producing) than sucrose** and is a main constituent of 'sugar-free' chewing gums. It is also added to many other conventional confectionery products to control their texture and prevent sugar crystallization. One disadvantage of sorbitol is that in high doses (50 g or more, a day) it produces a laxative effect (osmotic diarrhoea, for the technically minded). It is permitted for use in Australia, Belgium, Brazil, Canada, Denmark, Finland, France, Greece, Italy, Japan, Netherlands, Norway, South Africa, Spain, Sweden, Switzerland, UK, USA, and West Germany.

Mannitol (manna sugar)

Another polyol, which occurs in pumpkins, mushrooms, onions, beets, celery, and olives, mannitol is about half as sweet as sucrose. Its name derives from the fact that it is the main constituent of manna, the sweet exudate of the flowering ash tree of biblical renown. Like sorbitol, it is slowly and incompletely absorbed from the gut and so could have laxative properties, but in fact it is used in rather low concentrations, mainly in 'sugar-free' chewing gums as a dusting agent to assist in rolling and cutting the slabs. It is thought to be **relatively safe for teeth** and general health, but since it costs about ten times as much as sucrose (sorbitol costs less than twice as much) it seems unlikely to become a major constituent of confectionery. It is permitted for foods in Australia, Belgium, Canada, Denmark, France, Greece, Japan, South Africa, Spain, Sweden, Switzerland, UK, USA, and West Germany.

Xylitol

A polyol with about the same sweetness as sucrose (and twice that of sorbitol and mannitol), xylitol occurs widely in nature, for example in raspberries, yellow plums, endives, and lettuces. It is also formed in man as an intermediate product of glucose metabolism. Commercially it is produced from the wood of birch trees, and, because this is a process much more complicated than the simple extraction of sucrose from cane and beet, it is much more expensive and will remain so. In spite of this, interest in its commercial use has remained lively for several reasons. In extensive testing it has been found to produce no acid in plaque (some researchers even claim that it raises pH) and it is therefore currently regarded as **extremely safe for teeth**, though bacterial adaptation is not impossible. Secondly, it produces almost no impact on blood sugar levels, which is an advantage for diabetics (but bear in mind the caveat on calorific value of the 10–30 per cent which **is** absorbed in the gut – see sorbitol above). Thirdly, in spite of this poor absorption, the laxative effects of xylitol appear to be initially less than those of sorbitol or mannitol, and they reduce with repeated intake. Fourthly, it has a preservative effect against food spoilage micro-organisms about twice that of sucrose. And finally, xylitol has the remarkable property of producing a significant temperature drop when dissolved in the mouth, which adds to the interest of confectionery. For these reasons it is used in chewing gum, fruit gums, peppermints, and a few chocolates, especially in Finland. Its addition to ice-creams is expected, and its use as a preservative and taste improver in liquid medicines, in place of the ghastly sucrose and glucose syrups which abound, is to be warmly encouraged. It is permitted for use in Australia, Belgium, Finland, Greece, South Africa, Spain, Switzerland, UK, USA, and West Germany.

Palatinit® (isomalt)

This fairly new addition to the repertoire of sugar alcohol sweeteners is a commercially created mixture, with an impossibly long chemical name. It is fashioned by subjecting sucrose to a two-stage industrial process. Roughly speaking, this results in the production of derivatives of sorbitol and mannitol, and Palatinit is initially broken down in the gut to sorbitol, mannitol, and glucose. Its sweetness is about half that of sucrose, and initial tests suggest that it may be suitable as a sugar substitute to prevent dental decay. Its use in food has recently been approved in the UK.

NON-NUTRITIVE SWEETENERS

These are sometimes called 'the intense sweeteners' because they have a sweetness hundreds of times, and occasionally thousands of times, that of sucrose. Although a few of them are not absolutely non-nutritive (some, for example, are proteins) they are used in such small quantities as to make no significant contribution to nutrition.

While some intense sweeteners are extracted from natural products, others are entirely synthetic man-made compounds, which thought is apt to cause apprehension in the mind of the intelligent consumer. It is therefore worth remembering that extreme caution is now shown by governmental authorities in issuing or continuing the licence for any non-nutritive sweetener. Thus, the consumption of permitted sweeteners, both in manufactured foods, drinks, and pharmaceuticals, and at home in your tea, coffee, and cooking should not cause you any qualms. But note that non-nutritive sweeteners are specifically forbidden in many countries as additives in manufactured foods formulated for babies and young children.

Aspartame (Canderel®)

A sweetener made from two commercially produced amino

acids (L-phenylalanine and L-aspartic acid). The sweetness of this combination, first noticed in 1965, is about 200 times that of sucrose. In addition, the type of sweetness is regarded as closest to that of sucrose of all the non-nutritive sweeteners, with no bitter aftertaste. It is unstable at prolonged high temperature, and therefore not suitable for foods which are cooked or baked (though it may be added later where this is possible) and it is also unstable in strongly acid and neutral solutions, which limits its use in the soft drink industry. However, it is very suitable in tablet form for what is known in the business as a 'table-top' sweetener, for addition to tea, coffee, etc., and as such was first introduced in France in 1979. Between 1980 and 1981 the sales of these tablets increased six-fold, representing some 2000 tons of sugar equivalent. Since then it has been approved for use in the United Kingdom, where it can already be bought under the brand name Canderel. One tablet contains 18 mg of aspartame and has approximately the same sweetening power as a teaspoon of sucrose. Unfortunately, the current retail price is about ten times that of saccharine. It is regarded as extremely safe, since it undergoes normal protein metabolism in the body and **it produces no acid in plaque.** An acceptable daily intake of 40 mg per kg of body weight has been approved (compare with saccharine below), based on no effects at a hundred times that dose, and the Commissioner of the ultra-careful US Food and Drug Administration concluded that 'enormously large amounts of aspartame would have to be consumed by a normal individual before reaching even a cautiously estimated toxic threshold'.

Concern has been expressed in some circles that aspartame may be unsuitable for people suffering from the rare genetic disorder phenylketonuria (PKU) as they may not be able to metabolize the phenylalanine component, and in the United States a label is required on the packet drawing attention to this. However, even this caution may be over-zealous, since if a medium-sized (40 kg) child swallowed 40 tablets at once – equivalent in sweetness to half a pound of sugar – the phenylalanine levels in the blood would be the same as those produced by a quarter-pound hamburger! It is permitted for use in Algeria, Australia, Belgium, Brazil, Canada, Denmark, France, Ireland, Luxembourg, Mexico, Norway, Philippines, Singapore, South Africa, Sweden, Switzerland, Tunisia, UK, USA, and West Germany.

Acesulfame K

An organic salt (like saccharine), this new arrival on the sweetener scene has recently been approved in the UK. Its sweetness is about 150 times that of sucrose and it is extremely stable, both in food products and also in the human body, from which it is excreted unchanged. It has been claimed to reduce the growth and acid-producing capacity of *Streptococcus mutans* in dental plaque, but this is probably of academic interest only, since the levels of the compound required for sweetness in a product would not be high enough for this decay-inhibiting effect to be significant. It has a slightly bitter aftertaste, though not so much as that of saccharine. Acesulfame K is **extremely safe, for teeth** and for general health, and it is likely to have increasing use in soft drinks, calorie-reduced preserves and baked foods. It is under review in all the major industrialized nations, but is at the time of writing only approved for use in foods in the UK and for toothpastes in the USSR.

Saccharine

Discovered in 1879, its widespread use was promoted by sugar shortages during the First and Second World Wars. It is about 300 times as sweet as sucrose and is very stable, being eliminated from the body unchanged. Its stability in food and drink products, as well as its longevity in the field, has made it the most widely-used non-sugar sweetener in the world. Questions about its safety have periodically been raised, but evidence produced against this has not been strong enough to cause the revoking of product licences. However, the World Health Organisation suggests a **limit of 2.5 mg per day per each kilogram of body weight**. This is equivalent to 12 tablets for a 60 kg (131 lb = 9½ stone) adult, 8 tablets for a 40 kg (88 lb = 6 st 4 lb) child, 4 tablets for a 20 kg (44 lb = 3 st 2 lb) child, etc. The *Which?* report on sugar and other sweeteners (February 1979) states that one can of low-calorie drink will contain the equivalent of at least four saccharine tablets (12.5 mg each). It has a lingering taste and for some palates an unpleasant aftertaste, so in future it is likely to be used in combinations with other non-nutritive sweeteners, and eventually replaced by other products when their production costs fall relatively. It is **absolutely safe for teeth**, and the world's largest producer of saccharine in the USA is developing calcium saccharine as an alternative to the sodium salt in response to the growing concern about dietary sodium intake. Permitted for use in most countries.

Thaumatin (Talin®)

A low-calorie protein sweetener extracted from the West African katemfe fruit (*Thaumatoccus danielli*), some 2000–3000 times as sweet as sucrose. It has a delayed sweetness perception followed by a lingering taste, which seems to be ideal for masking the taste of liquid medicines and thereby reducing the sugar contents of these, as well as that of many foods and drinks. Its safety is thought to be extremely high (a safety factor of at least 80 000 times the expected daily intake) and it has recently been approved for use in foods in the UK, where its first application is expected to be in chewing gums. It is **perfectly safe for teeth**. So far it only approved for use in Japan and the UK but it is under review in all the major industrial nations.

Cyclamate

A calorie-free (= not decay-producing) sweetener discovered in 1937, about 25 times the sweetness of sucrose, with good stability (shelf-life) in various foods and drinks. It is frequently combined with saccharine, whose aftertaste it suppresses. It was banned in the UK in 1969, and the next year in the USA and Canada, following reports of toxicity in animals fed very large amounts over a two year period. It is now thought that the evidence against its general safety is doubtful, and in 1978 it was reintroduced in Canada. The main problem with cyclamate is its relatively low sweetening power, by comparison with other intensive sweeteners, requiring larger amounts than, for example, acesulfame K. That, and the fact that its main use is in soft drinks consumed in quantity by children, has caused the UK Food Additives and Contaminants Committee (1982) to conclude that it should not be restored to the permitted list. However, it is permitted in Austria, Belgium, Canada, Denmark, Finland, France, Ireland, Italy, Luxembourg, Netherlands, Norway, Portugal, Spain, Sweden, Switzerland, and West Germany.

Other new non-nutritive sweeteners

Many products are being developed to take part in the very competitive world market. Names which may become familiar include:

Stevioside – An extract from the leaves of the plant *Stevia rebaudiana* 120–240 times as sweet as sucrose, stable and used in a variety of foods and drinks in Japan.

Glycyrrhizin – An extract from liquorice roots, with a pronounced liquorice flavour, which when mixed in equal quantities with sucrose increases the sweetness 100 times. It is generally regarded as safe, is used for flavouring some pharmaceuticals, tobacco, and confectionery products, and is permitted for certain uses in Japan and the USA.

Neohesperidin dihydrochalcone (NeoDHC) – Synthesized from extracts of Seville oranges and other citrus fruit, variously reported as 350 to 2000 times as sweet as sugar, it enhances the sweetness of other sweeteners, with potential uses in chewing gum, confectionery, mouthwash, toothpaste, and some pharmaceuticals. It is approved in Belgium for soft drinks and chewing gum, and in Spain for pharmaceuticals.

Chloroderivatives of sucrose – These are being investigated, and one in particular, trichlorogalactosucrose (TGS), shows real promise, having a sweetness 500–600 times that of sucrose, virtually no aftertaste or lingering sweetness, greater stability than sucrose over a wide range of conditions and no susceptibility to digestive or bacterial enzymes (i.e. it is safe for teeth). A comprehensive series of toxicological tests is in progress.

Extracts of the West African miracle fruit (miraculin – a taste modifier) and of serendipity berries (monellin) seem less promising than at first, because of lingering taste effects and limited stability respectively.

Cynarin – Another natural taste modifier, may have a future because it doesn't last so long. It is found in globe artichokes, which have apparently been used for years by canny French parents in the main course to make the following dessert taste sweeter than it actually is.

Mixtures of sweeteners

A recent trend in the field of sweeteners has been called 'the multiple sweetener approach'. It has been found that the sweetening power of, say, saccharine/aspartame mixtures is greater, by as much as 50 per cent, than their separate sweetnesses added together. This 'synergistic effect' has the advantage that lower total concentrations of sweeteners will be needed to produce a particular level of sweetness, resulting in lower costs and even greater safety factors. Already aspartame/saccharine mixtures with less aftertaste are being marketed in the more popular diet cola drinks, where rapid sales are expected, and therefore the limited shelf-life of aspartame in solution would not be a problem.

Conclusion

In view of the facts that non-sugar sweeteners are specifically forbidden in many countries as additives in manufactured foods formulated for babies and young children, and that sugars are not only unnecessary in the diet but also potentially bad for general as well as dental health, it is to be hoped that the levels of sweetness demanded by popular taste will fall – notwithstanding the efforts of the confectionery manufacturers in the opposite direction. This is possible. The total sugar consumption per capita during 1981 was 53.4 kg in Australia, 49.3 kg in New Zealand, 46.7 kg in the USSR, 38.8 kg in the EEC countries, 38.7 kg in the USA – but it was only 8.0 kg in India, 4.1 kg in China and 1.7 kg in Bangladesh. The rates of dental decay in different countries correspond closely with sugar consumption.

CAUTION ON LABELLING

Because of the increasing awareness of the dangers to health of sugar in the diets of affluent countries, and the consequent demand for foods and drinks of low calorific value, much effort, as we have seen, is being put into development of safer alternatives. But just as the regulations affecting their use varies between different countries, so does the labelling of manufactured foodstuffs. One of the results of this is a certain amount of confusion, and the descriptions on food labels are sometimes deceptive.

At worst, the terms 'sugarless' and 'sugar-free' may be used merely to signify the absence of sucrose in a product loaded with glucose or high-fructose corn syrup and therefore bad for the teeth. More difficult to spot is the application of these terms to products sweetened with the sugar alcohols (also called polyols and polyhydric alcohols). This description is chemically correct, and would also imply relative safety for teeth, but, where low calorific value is implied, it would be entirely misleading. If you see the description 'sucrose-free' on a food or drink, look for mention of monosaccharide, glucose, fructose, isoglucose, maltose (or almost any other -ose), starch syrup, corn syrup, high fructose corn syrup (HFCS) and invert sugar or honey. All of these are fattening and **bad for the teeth.**

7

How to clean your teeth and your children's teeth

In addition to sugar control, the most important thing you can do to help your children keep their teeth is to train them to remove plaque. In learning how to do this you will improve the life span of your own teeth as well. (The mechanism of gum disease will be considered in a later chapter called 'Plaque and gum disease' – p.122).

As I said in Chapter 2, plaque forms all the time on any hard surface in the mouth – teeth, fillings, crowns and bridges, dentures, and even on the hard material deposited on the teeth, which the layman calls tartar and the dentist **calculus**. Your job is to get the plaque off all these hard surfaces, and to show your children, when they are old enough, how to get it off for themselves. The problem is that plaque, being colourless and nearly transparent is very difficult to see.

DYES

One of the greatest developments in the prevention both of decay and gum disease in the last decade has been the increasing use of harmless dyes which show up plaque. Without these, trying to remove plaque is rather like looking for the Emperor's new clothes in Hans Andersen's story – you can't see it. Dentists used to tell patients to clean their teeth, but had no good way of showing them how to do so. With the advent of the plaque dyes, the picture became transformed. These dyes are available as liquids or tablets and are called **disclosing solutions** and **disclosing**

tablets because they show up or disclose plaque in the mouth. They are harmless food colourings, the sort used to colour icing on cakes. Most chemists (drug stores) now stock disclosing tablets, and some have the liquids. These special dental products are not very expensive, but, if you want to save money, a simple food dye will do the job just as well. Tablets are more convenient to use, which is a consideration since it is a good idea to make the fiddly business of plaque removal as easy as possible.

SHOPPING LIST

To learn how to clean your teeth you should have ready the following things:

New toothbrush, nylon, small head, medium hardness
Box of dental floss, waxed
Small pocket torch
Bottle of food colouring, or packet of disclosing tablets
Vaseline (petroleum jelly)
Bathroom mirror

BRUSHING YOUR TEETH

Procedure for brushing

I am going to write this in some detail, but, because you can't be reading a complicated description at the same time as brushing, I will provide a check-list at the end which you can use in the bathroom.

1. Clean your teeth. What you are going to look for is the plaque you usually miss. If you wear a denture, it's better to take this out first, so that all the tooth surfaces are exposed.
2. Put a thin smear of vaseline on your lips to stop the dye reaching them.
3. Put a disclosing tablet in your mouth (or a teaspoon of

food colouring), chew it up and swish the liquid around your mouth to cover all the tooth surfaces, without swallowing (the dye is harmless if swallowed but you need it in your mouth, not your stomach). Then spit it out into the basin.

4. Rinse the unattached dye out of your mouth.

5. With the aid of your pocket torch and the bathroom mirror have a look in your mouth. For the purpose of description I am assuming the use of a red dye. Here is what you will see:

Your gums, tongue, and inside cheeks will be bright red – don't worry, this will wear off within a couple of hours, or by the morning if you are doing this experiment before going to bed.

Your teeth will be white, very faint pink, and dark pink. Where they are **white** the tooth surface is clean. Where they are **faintly pink**, they are covered with a thin protein layer – the forerunner of plaque (not everyone shows this). And where there are patches of proper **pink**, they are covered with plaque.

The most common places to find plaque are **recessed surfaces** where the brush has skidded over without touching:

— next to the gum
— where adjacent teeth meet
— holes in teeth
— gaps around the edges of fillings
— on the surface of calculus (this is not recessed, but it is rough, and the plaque sticks to it better).

6. Now take your toothbrush, **without toothpaste** which would confuse the picture, and put the bristles on some plaque. Press the bristles quite hard into the plaque, and **jiggle** the brush slightly back and forth in any direction, maintaining the pressure. You will see that the plaque comes off easily because it is soft. It was there because your brush missed it on previous brushings.

If you are brushing next to the gum, you may notice

71

that it has started to bleed. **Don't be alarmed**. It simply means that your gums are inflamed, which is common before you have learned to remove plaque. It also means that, by cleaning your teeth properly, you are taking the first steps towards curing gum disease. Within a week, your gums will have stopped bleeding when you brush them, showing that they are on the mend.

7. The accessible areas most often missed by the brush are the tongue side of the lower teeth, behind the last teeth in either jaw, and the surfaces facing gaps, if you have had any teeth extracted. Right-handed people can clean the teeth on the left side of their mouth more easily, and vice versa.

8. The easiest way to remove plaque from around the gum margin is to put the brush half on the tooth and half on the gum, angled as if to push the gum down the tooth. There is no evidence that it actually does push back the gum. Rather the opposite is true – the healthy, plaque-free gum is more likely to stay at the same level than gum constantly in contact with plaque. Another advantage of positioning the brush partly on the gum is that you can feel exactly where the bristles are and where they have already been.

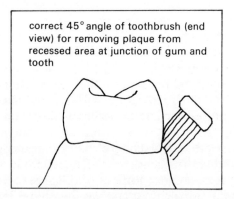

correct 45° angle of toothbrush (end view) for removing plaque from recessed area at junction of gum and tooth

Fig. 10. Position of toothbrush for making the gums healthy.

9. One limitation of complete cleaning is that people imagine that the handle of the brush should always be pointing forwards out of their mouth. To get to the **backs of the last teeth** in each jaw, you must hold your brush out sideways, pushing back the corner of your mouth, with the bristles coming at the tooth from behind. This sideways position is also useful for getting into any gaps where back teeth have been lost.

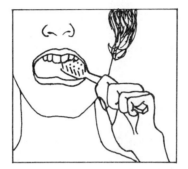

Fig. 11. Position of toothbrush for cleaning behind the back teeth.

10. When you are cleaning the **tongue side of the lower front teeth** (if you open your mouth wide and tilt your head forward you'll be able to see these surfaces in the mirror), the best way to hold the brush is with the handle pointing **forwards, but angled steeply up,** the sort of angle at which soldiers on parade carry flags when marching.

11. Using your bathroom mirror and torch, you ought to be able to check the lower teeth inside and out until you have removed the last traces of visible plaque.

12. **Mouth mirrors** – When it comes to the upper teeth a difficulty presents itself. Because of the geometry of the head and the presence of the upper front teeth, you cannot see the inner surfaces of the upper teeth in your bathroom mirror. With what you have learnt from brushing your lower teeth, and from the feel of the

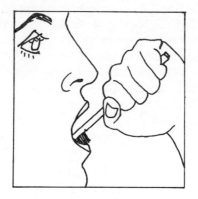

Fig. 12. Fist grip for cleaning insides of lower front teeth.

brush on the gum it should be possible to make sure that you haven't left any plaque. But, if you really want to see for yourself, you will need a second mirror. Any small cosmetic or handbag mirror will do very well for the purpose, though the round ones on long handles which dentists use are best. If you are very persuasive, your dentist might agree to sell you one of his metal mirrors (make sure it is not an old scratched one). Alternatively, he can obtain cheap plastic ones from the manufacturers and sell them to you. Or you can buy them at some chemists.

Using your mirror takes a little practice. You stand in front of your bathroom mirror and hold the mouth mirror inside your mouth next to the tooth you want to look at. Tilting it this way and that, you will find a position where you can see what you want to see by double reflection. This sounds complicated, but you will quickly get the knack. It is the same principle as using two mirrors to look at the back of your head.

With the aid of this second mirror, and your pocket torch, check that you have removed all the plaque, looking specially at the back teeth. If any remains, remove it.

Fig. 13. Using a mouth mirror and bathroom mirror to see behind the top teeth.

Brushing technique

I haven't said much about what brushing technique you should use because I don't really think it is important. Some dentists recommend rolling the bristles from the gum surface on to the tooth. I mentioned pressing against the plaque and jiggling the brush. These two techniques even have names – the 'roll technique' and the 'Bass technique' – and there are others. What is important is that you get the plaque off, and **any method that suits you and works is good**. The usual tooth brushing method, long scrubbing strokes against the outside of the teeth, doesn't work so well because it leaves plaque behind. It has one other disadvantage, too. If your gums have receded past the end of the hard enamel, the scrubbing technique gradually wears notches in the softer dentine of the necks of those teeth, especially if you use a hard brush. After many years of this, with a bit more gum recession, the notches may become so deep that

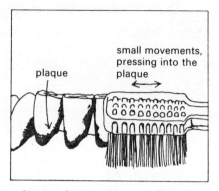

Fig. 14. Brushing technique – use small jiggling movements
pushing against the tooth, not long sweeps.

the teeth start to look like half-felled trees. This usually
doesn't matter to the teeth, but it may look unsightly, and it
makes them more difficult to clean. People with this
problem are well-intentioned but ill-informed. They have
used a tremendous amount of physical force and enthusiasm
in tooth-brushing, when what they needed was accuracy.

ACCURACY IS THE KEY TO PLAQUE REMOVAL

Visualizing your teeth – the mental image

For the purposes of tooth-brushing most people imagine
their teeth as two curved walls of tooth, of which they have
to brush the two sides and the top. In reality those walls are
made of individual teeth, each of which has a front, a back,
two sides, and a top – **five surfaces for each tooth. The only
way to stop dental disease is to clean all of them**. One of my
patients who was very keen to learn about plaque control
and was very quick on the uptake, came back to let me
check her progress. She said, 'I feel I know each of my teeth
personally'. That remark perfectly expresses the detail of
visualization needed for the job in hand.

How long does it take to brush your teeth properly?

Most people imagine they brush their teeth for about two minutes each time, whereas in my experience they actually do it for about thirty seconds. To brush teeth properly takes a lot longer than two minutes at first, say, something like five minutes. Later, as you become more skilful, this may reduce by a minute or two. However, the object is not to brush for a certain length of time, but to remove the plaque. You will discover how long it takes by looking.

Now, even four minutes feels like an amazingly long time to brush when you are used to thirty seconds. If you don't **look** to see what effect you are having, it can also be extremely **boring**. This is another reason why disclosing dyes have made such a difference. Instead of toothbrushing being some vague magic ritual against the evil spirits of tooth decay and gum disease, the disclosing of plaque has made plaque removal a logical, observable procedure with a definite end.

How long should you go on using the dye?

The answer is simple – use it every two or three days until you consistently find that you have no plaque, back teeth as well as front, inside as well as out, after you have cleaned your teeth. After that, go back to the dye once a month when you are in a critical frame of mind to check that your standards haven't dropped. (Note that if you use the dye every day, it may accumulate on the gums and give them an unnatural colour.)

Maintaining standards

As you become more expert in what to look for, and you start to notice your gums getting tighter and paler pink (less inflamed) and as they stop bleeding and you become used to a very clean feeling in your mouth, there will be a sense of

77

achievement and 'oral well being', which ought to encourage you. However, your initial enthusiasm is apt to wane over the months and your plaque removal become less thorough.

One day you may notice that there is some blood on your toothbrush again. So you know that you have to raise your standards, go back to using the dye (if you have stopped) and concentrate more until you have cured the bleeding.

What about sensitivity of the teeth when you brush them?

This may happen when your gums recede below the edge of the enamel, which is insensitive, exposing the top part of the root. The cause is related to acid attack by plaque. In its absence the newly exposed root surface will pick up minerals from saliva, and any initial sensitivity will quickly disappear. If plaque and sugar are present, the resulting acid will demineralize the exposed root, and sensitivity persist. The way to deal with this is to endure the pain of brushing and make sure you get all the plaque off. Within a couple of days the pain will be much reduced as remineralization takes place. You can assist this by spitting out but not rinsing with water after brushing and by rubbing a little fluoride toothpaste on the sensitive area with your finger and leaving it there. 'Desensitizing' toothpastes are marketed, but they are probably no better than ordinary fluoride toothpaste, left on, and they are very expensive.

If tooth neck sensitivity is so severe that you can't bring yourself to brush thoroughly, dentists have special solutions and varnishes which they can apply to the necks of the teeth, but these are only available through dental supply companies.

Sometimes teeth become sensitive after a dentist or dental hygienist has 'scaled' them, that is scraped off the layers of calculus. Usually it is the lower front teeth, which are the thinnest and accumulate most calculus. Removing this is like taking off an overcoat, and the thin necks of the teeth may be sensitive to cold air. With good plaque removal this will get better quickly. It will get better with poor plaque removal too, as more calculus is formed and the coat goes back on.

That concludes what I know about brushing teeth. Now we have the check-list for brushing so that you can try it out.

Bathroom check-list for brushing your teeth

1. Clean teeth first.
2. Vaseline lips.
3. Dye into mouth, swish around.
4. Rinse with water.
5. Look for plaque (bathroom mirror and torch).
6. Remove plaque, with brush angled at 45° to the gum.
7. Start with easy areas, e.g. front teeth, to learn how much pressure needed. Jiggle, don't scrub.
8. Then move to inner surfaces of lower back teeth. Then outer, then biting surfaces.
9. Clean outer and biting surfaces of upper teeth.
10. With small mirror, look at the inner surfaces of the upper teeth, by double reflection.
11. Lower front teeth, inner surfaces, are reached with handle pointing forwards and angled up (fist grip).
12. Behind the last back teeth reached by pulling handle sideways out of corner of mouth, bristles pointing forwards.
13. Bleeding should not alarm you, but it does indicate previously poor brushing in that area.

Suggestion

You should try to master toothbrushing before going on the next section which describes the use of dental floss. This will give you some confidence to continue. Dentists rarely attempt to explain toothbrushing and flossing at the same appointment and with good reason. It is, for most people, just too much to absorb, even under the ideal conditions of one-to-one teaching. How much more difficult it must be to follow from the printed page. Once you have become good at using the toothbrush, however, learning to handle floss will be easier, because your visualization of the teeth will be better.

DENTAL FLOSS

As I said, floss is probably even more important than the toothbrush. This is because one of the commonest sites for decay is where neighbouring teeth touch, and the worst gum disease takes place between the teeth, where the brush cannot reach.

Now, explaining **on paper** how to use floss is notoriously difficult. This is because describing positions and move-ments of parts of the body, in this case the hands and mouth, is difficult. Demonstrating them is easy, as when a dentist or hygienist shows a patient what to do, but I have been told by several experts in oral hygiene instruction that they have yet to see a satisfactory printed explanation of the use of floss. Some said, 'don't even try – it will put the reader off reading your book'.

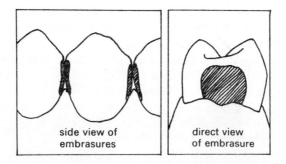

Fig. 15. Embrasures cannot be reached by a toothbrush.

But, because floss is so important, and because this is a self-help book, I must try. And I must therefore ask you, challenge you perhaps, to make a considerable effort to follow the ensuing explanation.

To begin I shall introduce a technical word which will make the method easier to follow. The surfaces of next-door teeth (the teeth which face each other) are called **embrasures** (em-**bray**-sures). These are the areas where the brush cannot reach because the teeth are too close together. Floss, however, can be passed completely between even the tightest contacts.

Dental floss is a thread of tiny man-made fibres (in the old days silk fibres were used), which can be bought in any chemist (drug store) and most supermarkets. It comes on a reel in a plastic box, or bottle, which has a small raised half-punched piece of metal, against which you will pull the floss to cut it. Two sorts are available, waxed and unwaxed. The unwaxed may be fractionally better at removing plaque. The waxed type is much easier to handle, and I suggest you use this.

Techniques for using floss

There are two ways of using floss. In one, you wind the two ends of a piece around your fingers and pass the middle section between the teeth. People become quite good at this, but I think it is easier to use the **loop method**, which I shall now describe.

Cut off a piece of floss about ten inches (25 cm) long. Tie it into a loop. With waxed floss an ordinary reef knot or thumb knot will slip. I suggest bending your piece of floss in the middle so that you have the two ends lying along side each other, tie a simple thumb knot and pull it tight.

Then simply repeat the process and pull the second one tight.

Pull open the loop – the knots will run together and then stop slipping. You now have a loop about three inches across.

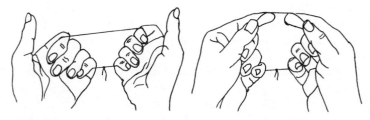

Fig. 17.

Hold it between your hands with the fingers inside and the thumbs free.

Put your index fingers under the top strand and straighten them. The thumbs may be moved over to hold the floss.

Pull your hands apart to make the whole loop taut. The part of the loop between your index fingers must be kept very short, for maximum control. Turning the index fingers towards you, and keeping the loop taut, push the loop down between any two lower back teeth. A mirror will help you position the floss. In it you will see what is shown in Fig. 18.

Remember:
1. The loop must be small so that your hands are close together
2. You must not let the loop go slack
3. You must keep your index fingers very close together
4. Keep your thumbs outside the mouth.

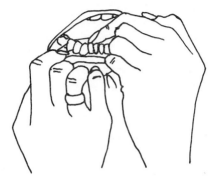

Fig. 18.

If you have difficulty in getting the floss between the teeth, check in the mirror to see that the angle of the floss is right so that it can pass between them. If it is still difficult, move the floss from side to side pushing down, and 'zig-zag' it past the tight contact. You now have the floss lying in the embrasure area with the gum below. Your job is to use the floss to scrape the surfaces of the embrasures front and back. First pull it forward, keeping the tension, on to the back of the tooth nearest the front of your mouth; and scrape it up and down a couple of times (not from side to side). Now push it against the front of the tooth behind (the embrasure back) and repeat the scraping procedure.

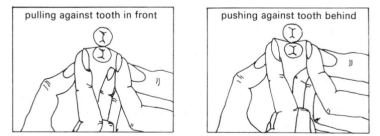

Fig. 19. Cleaning both embrasures – scrape with the floss up and down, not side to side.

Slide the floss out from between the teeth and have a look at it. You may see any of the following things on the floss:

1. Blood – This means you have gum inflammation in that space.
2. Plaque – If you have used a dye, this will be coloured.
3. Bits of food (floss is good at this) – This usually means that a filling doesn't contact the next door tooth properly, which you should mention to your dentist.
4. The floss is badly frayed, or even broken – You have a filling, or fillings, in that embrasure which are very rough or have ledges. Sometimes they even prevent the floss passing down between the teeth. Sometimes it goes in, but won't come out. In any of these situations, you should go to your dentist and ask him to deal with the problem, because anything which stops you flossing in a particular area allows gum disease to continue there.

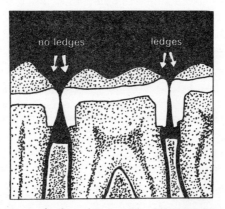

Fig. 20. Diagram of a dental X-ray. The filling surfaces on the left can be flossed, those on the right can't.

Now try the same procedure with your lower front teeth, and then with the rest of your lower back teeth.

When it comes to the upper teeth, it is easier to alter the hold on the floss. Hold the same loop across the right finger, but instead of using the left finger, switch to the left thumb as seen in the diagram. This will do for the **left** upper teeth. When it comes to the right teeth, reverse the hold to the left finger and right thumb. Keep them close together and the floss taut at all times. Your elbow can fall against your body in a relaxed position. Clean both embrasures of each space.

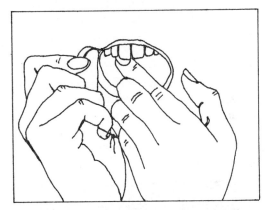

Fig. 21. Comfortable hold for flossing the top teeth using index finger and thumb.

Now that you have experimented with holding the floss and passing it between various tooth contacts, adopt a routine to make sure that every embrasure is scraped. Start at the back of the last tooth on one side, upper or lower, where there is no tooth contact, and work your way forward going into each embrasure and cleaning both surfaces, including where teeth are missing, until you reach the middle of the front teeth. Then either carry on round, or start behind the last tooth on the other side and work forward. Do the same for the other jaw.

Flossing with one hand

If you, or a member of your family, only has the use of one hand, through bad arthritis or for other reasons, the above technique for floss will be irrelevant. There are special floss holders which can be used. Ask your dentist to get one for you from a dental supply company.

Ledges (also called overhangs)

When you are starting to become acquainted with your teeth you will recognize which fillings have ledges that cause the floss to fray or break, and be able to point them out to your dentist.

Sometimes it is possible to smooth the ledges directly. Other times the best answer is to replace the filling, taking care to use wooden or plastic wedges to prevent the ledges from recurring. By replacing one filling, ledges on adjacent teeth can also be smoothed. It is very important that you have ledges dealt with, because they are a major cause of gum disease, and ultimately of losing teeth.

Can floss do harm?

Yes it can, if you have very tight contacts between the teeth and push the floss very hard. When it finally whips through, it will hit the gum like a cheese-cutting wire, and with a similar effect. That is why I say you should zig-zag the floss through tight contacts. What, if on removing it, part of a filling flicks out? That is good news, in a sense, because the filling was very loose and needed replacing anyhow. Loose fillings are quite dangerous because decay goes on underneath them.

Initially the flossing may cause bleeding if you have gum disease, but don't worry about this. The bleeding will stop after a few days, providing that you don't have rough fillings, and this will tell you that your plaque removal is working.

How long does flossing take?

At first it may take you something like five minutes to floss all the embrasures, because you will find handling the floss and finding the spaces awkward. And this five minutes flossing must be added on to the five minutes brushing. This is a considerable length of time, if you have only been used to the usual thirty seconds casual brushing. To embark on something twenty times as long, and to have to concentrate on what you are doing, requires an enormous change in behaviour and motivation. Also, this change will have to be permanent, because plaque control is a lifelong requirement if you want to save your teeth. This change in cleaning your teeth from what had been automatic behaviour is the most difficult part. Only you can decide if the increased effort and attention is worth it: to avoid dentures, reduce the number of your visits to the dentist, save money, and have sweet breath and a clean feeling in your mouth. For an adult, it can transform your dental future from one where you are likely to lose a great many teeth by the end of your life, to one where you may not lose any.

Flossing will become easier, of course. Your flossing time will drop to something like two minutes, if your fillings are smooth, and your brushing time will fall below five as you become an expert in finding plaque. And, if you get used to the feeling of a clean mouth and tight gums, you will become intolerant of having plaque on the teeth, so motivation will develop. But you have to reach that stage first, which is difficult and tedious.

DENTISTS DO DISCRIMINATE

There is one other factor to be borne in mind. Rightly or wrongly, dentists do discriminate between patients. They tend to work harder to save clean mouths than dirty ones. Partly this is an emotional reaction to what they see, but partly it is logical as well. It doesn't make a great deal of sense to spend hours patching up mouths in which disease is continuing unchecked.

I was told a story once about an old test used in Cornwall

to assess madness. The story goes that the patient was placed in a room which had a tap running into a blocked sink, with the water pouring all over the floor. Also in the room was a bucket and a mop. If the patient turned off the tap before mopping the floor, he was regarded as sane. If he mopped the floor without turning off the tap, he was regarded as insane. By that assessment, doing dentistry in a plaque-filled sugar-soaked mouth is insane.

HOW MANY TIMES A DAY SHOULD THE TEETH BE CLEANED?

Research shows that if all plaque were removed completely every 48 hours, this would control gum disease in most people. It would have to be much more frequent to control decay. The concensus view is that for most people twice a day is enough, because plaque removal is often not perfect, and there is a possibility that what you miss in the morning you will remove in the evening. Cleaning more often won't do any harm, provided you don't scrub the teeth and don't brush immediately after acid foods or drinks. Flossing every other day should be adequate once you have restored the gums to a state of health – no bleeding when you floss.

As to the best times to clean the teeth, it is more sensible to clean your teeth **before** a meal rather than after it. By doing this, you remove the bacteria which turn sugar into acid. Also cleaning your teeth last thing at night is advisable because of the reduced saliva flow during sleep. So, if you are only going to clean your teeth twice a day, the best advice would be before breakfast and last thing at night.

AN APPLE A DAY?

The British Dental Association and other dental organizations, used to advocate the eating of apples for dental health. As tooth cleaning tools they are not very good, because they do not reach to the recessed areas of the tooth surface. The same applies to raw carrots and celery. Only something which can be pressed directionally into the recessed areas will remove plaque from them. Apples, carrots, and celery also contain some sugar, and apples are acid, so they probably shouldn't be eaten after brushing the teeth at night. They can never be a substitute for flossing and brushing. But while they are not good for cleaning teeth, they are wonderful substitutes for sweets and soft drinks as a snack. Some recent research suggests that if you finish a meal with a little cheese, this reduces acid production in the plaque.

CLEANING CHILDREN'S TEETH

The best method for cleaning a child's teeth will vary according to the age of the child, but certain general points are worth bearing in mind:

(1) All children need a lot of physical contact with their parents, and cleaning thier teeth can become a satisfying part of this. Later on, toothbrushing may have warm and comfortable associations.
(2) Don't think that you are usurping the dentist's role by looking and feeling in children's mouths. Taking a detailed interest in what is happening there can only help the dentist.
(3) When supervising older children in cleaning their own teeth, giving praise and making it fun is likely to be more productive than being negative and fault-finding.
(4) You need to develop the ability to see into the mouth at the same time as wielding an instrument (brush, mirror, torch).
(5) Don't rely on children to remove all the plaque. Often they cannot do it completely till about the age of eight. But let them take part in the activity as early as they wish, so that it is not merely something done to them.

Babies

From the time when the first teeth come through at about six months (by the way, there is a lot of variation in this, so don't worry if they are late), the teeth can be cleaned gently with a 'cotton bud' or small piece of gauze. You can do this most easily kneeling beside your bed with the baby lying on it, or else with the baby lying on your lap. Your normal nappy-changing position is most suitable. Use your fingers gently to hold back the cheek when looking at the outer surfaces of the 'cheek teeth'.

1–3 years

About this time it is a good idea to start using a children's toothbrush, with a small head and medium bristles. **Use a very small quantity of fluoride toothpaste** – the size of a small pea on the end of the brush. If you think the child finds the taste too strong, use a milder one or a special children's toothpaste. If you would like to use dye to check your plaque removal, use a cotton bud dipped in food colouring, and rub it round the teeth. Food colouring is tasteless and harmless, so the child can swallow what doesn't stick to the plaque. Your pocket torch can help you see. Keep an eye out for changes in colour on parts of the teeth, which may be a sign of decay.

After cleaning the teeth, you can let your child play with the brush, perhaps while having a bath. Even if he, or she, only chews or sucks it, this helps the child get used to the feeling and allows him or her to imitate what you do in your own mouth. Imitation is an important part of early development, and children like to participate in family routines. If, when the child is a little older, the family gathers in the bathroom for a toothbrushing session, it will seem like fun, and is less likely to become regarded as a chore.

When the child stands easily, a good position for you to adopt is kneeling, the child standing with his back to you, head and shoulders laid back against you to one side, so that you can look into his mouth as the dentist does. When he gets taller, this can be changed to a position where you sit and the child stands between your legs, leaning back on to you. One of the advantages of these positions is that the child is being cuddled while this is going on. Also you have good control of the head. The cheeks can be pulled gently aside with your fingers, from behind.

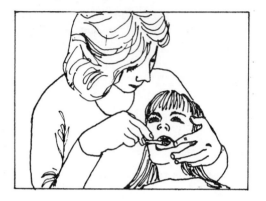

Fig. 22. Good position for cleaning a child's teeth.

4–5 years

Depending on your interest, this may be the time to start using a disclosing solution or tablet. The child will be able to rinse out properly. Disclosing need not be a routine event, because all you are using it for is to check that you have removed plaque, and after a couple of weeks you will be sure of your technique. In any case, don't use it every day. If you saturate a cotton bud with dye and move it around the teeth, inside and out, the dye will flow all over the teeth.

Also at this time the child will probably take over more of his own brushing, but you must continue to check it afterwards, and finish the job if necessary.

Remember that if a child wants to look in the bathroom mirror you will either have to set one down to his level, or else provide a box for him to stand on.

6–7 years

Around this age children, becoming more independent, may wish to look for plaque themselves, so the use of disclosing dyes will be necessary. I think it is helpful if you allow your children to look for disclosed plaque in your mouth as well as their own. It is always easier to see in someone else's mouth, and this makes visualization of the teeth and gums more complete. They may help you find plaque, too.

Checking the effectiveness of children's brushing should continue until you are confident that they are doing an excellent job every time. After that, periodic spot checks should be made, which will also permit you to keep an eye on the teeth for signs of decay, and notice the permanent teeth coming through.

An important stage is reached when the first permanent molars erupt behind the baby teeth at an age from 5½ onwards. This will mean that you and the child must clean further back in the mouth than before. It is particularly important to preserve these teeth, and they are the most prone to decay.

Flossing for children

There is some disagreement in dental circles about the appropriateness of using floss on children's teeth. Control of decay is mainly achieved by diet control and fluoride (for recommended fluoride dosage see p.112, and few children have destructive gum disease. In addition, the manual dexterity of children below their teens is often not good enough to manipulate floss. Some adults can find it difficult. Perhaps the best advice to give is that flossing can be started by parents, for the sake of children's gums, in areas where fillings have been placed **which go down the side of a tooth in the embrasures** (what dentists call Class 2 fillings). It must be up to you to decide when and if your child is interested and able to use floss effectively. It is not recommended for baby teeth, whose crowns are shorter, and whose gums are higher. With these it may hurt the gums, and anyway the mouth is probably too small.

SUMMARY ON PLAQUE REMOVAL

1. To learn how to remove plaque you have to be able to see it. For this you need a dye. Learn in your own mouth first. Then you can help your children.
2. Plaque is soft and easily removed once you have reached it.
3. Each tooth has five surfaces, three of which can be reached with a brush. Floss can reach the other two, the **embrasures**.
4. Baby teeth should not be flossed because of the high gum level. Children's permanent teeth which have fillings in the embrasures should be flossed. Most adults need to floss all their embrasures, once a day until gum disease stops, then every other day.
5. Clean babies' teeth with a cotton bud or cotton gauze. Nappy-changing position. Use fingers to hold back the cheeks so you can see. Work in a good light.
6. Progress to a brush at 1–2 years old. Let the child play with it.
7. Encourage imitation, work in the 'cuddle position', use small amounts of a mild toothpaste with fluoride, make it fun and give praise rather than criticism.
8. Food dye can be applied to children's teeth with a cotton bud. The unattached dye can be swallowed safely. When older the child will be able to rinse out.
9. Children usually need routine help with their plaque removal until age 7 or 8. After that, spot checks with

dye are enough. When you check their plaque removal, let them check yours.

10. There is no fixed time for which you need to clean your teeth. You stop when all the plaque is off. This you can tell only by looking, not assuming.

11. Teeth do not bleed, gums do. Not having bleeding while brushing means either you have been doing it well, and the gums are healthy, or else so badly that the brush doesn't get anywhere near the gums to make them bleed.

8

Toothbrushes, toothpaste, and other products

TOOTHBRUSHES

Most people use the same toothbrush for months on end, and long after it is really useful. The typical purchase rate is thought to be one toothbrush per person per year. Bearing in mind that **accuracy** is what is needed, it follows that as soon as toothbrush bristles become permanently bent, you can no longer aim them properly at the recessed areas of the tooth.

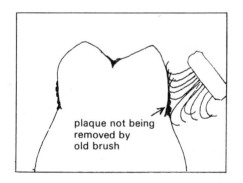

plaque not being
removed by
old brush

Fig. 23. Only straight bristles will dislodge plaque.

With brushing taking several minutes each time, the useful life of a toothbrush is usually **less than a month**. It therefore makes sense to buy several toothbrushes for each member of the family, to put in store, so that you can throw away any which are worn out, and not hang on to them because you forgot to add them to your shopping list.

WHAT SORT SHOULD YOU BUY?

There are different opinions about this, and manufacturers make many claims. However, I don't think it makes much difference provided you follow certain rules:

1. The head of the toothbrush should be **small** so that you can manoeuvre it easily at different angles. Buying children's brushes, even for adults to use, meets this requirement and it is a bit cheaper, though the handles may be too small for an adult with big hands. Those toothbrushes with very long heads, which look as if they could clean half your teeth with one stroke are not much good.

2. Buy **nylon** rather than natural bristle. They are generally cheaper and last longer. They dry out faster, and don't become as soft as natural bristle. Some people have a prejudice in favour of anything natural rather than man-made. With hairbrushes, natural bristles **are** better because they have scales which help clean the hair. But with toothbrushes, man-made fibres are better – not on day one but a week or so later.

3. Do not buy toothbrushes labelled 'soft'. The bristles need to be fairly rigid to dislodge plaque, and anyway they will soften with age. '**Medium**', or even 'hard' if you like the feeling, will be better. Exceptions to this occur when a dentist recommends a soft brush for a few days after gum surgery, if the gums feel tender.

That's all really. If a manufacturer advertises a special 'plaque removing' brush, it doesn't mean much. That is what all brushes are supposed to do. The idea of rounded ends to bristles advertised by some manufacturers is probably unnecessary because cut ends quickly become rounded in use, and there is no evidence they do any harm. Provided you follow the three rules above, just buy the cheapest brushes you can find, and plenty of them.

SPECIAL BRUSHES

Interest in effective tooth cleaning is increasing, and so is the potential market for new tooth cleaning products. There are many gimmicks about, but also some quite useful additions to the normal range of toothbrushes. One of the best is the single tuft brush which several manufacturers produce. This brush has an extremely small head which fits quite easily in to the space from which a tooth has been lost to clean the adjacent surfaces. Another advantage is that it can be used in areas like the tongue side of the lower back teeth, where some people find an ordinary toothbrush makes them feel sick.

Very small tapering 'bottle brushes' which look rather like tiny Christmas trees, are also useful for cleaning out medium size spaces between teeth. They are sold as a handle with several replacement heads. Floss is just as effective for this purpose but some dentists recommend bottle brushes.

Denture cleaning brushes are also available. They are a little like nail brushes but with a large extra-long tuft of thick bristles on the other side. These long bristles are better than an ordinary toothbrush at reaching the awkward or fiddly bits on the inside of some dentures. Incidentally you should learn to clean a denture in a similar way to cleaning teeth, by using a food dye (in the liquid form). You are trying to do the same thing – remove plaque.

Finally, many manufacturers make 'travelling' tooth-brushes, which can be carried in a hand-bag, briefcase, etc. These have a head which lives inside the handle, and can be pulled out, reversed, and pushed into the handle for use. They have advantages for two groups of people. First, the real tooth cleaning enthusiasts who have become so used to the beautiful smooth feeling of clean teeth that they tend to brush their teeth at work at some point during the day. Secondly, the much thicker handle is a real help to arthritis sufferers and others who can't close their hands properly around the handle of an ordinary brush. The handles of travelling toothbrushes are ventilated to allow the bristles to dry out between uses.

IMPORTANT NOTE: If you have had a fixed bridge fitted to replace a missing tooth or teeth, cleaning around the supporting roots is made more difficult by the fact that the 'teeth' are joined together. It is essential that you get the dentist to show you how to clean under the join so as to prevent gum disease and reduce the likelihood of decay. The little 'bottle brushes' may come in handy and there are special types of floss and floss threaders.

WHAT ABOUT ELECTRIC TOOTHBRUSHES?

Electric toothbrushes have motors which make the head rotate rapidly back and forth. I think they have three advantages and four disadvantages.

The advantages are: they have very small heads, they are fun for children to use and they can help people with limited wrist movement or control, such as the elderly or handicapped. Only in the last instance will they be any better at plaque removal.

The disadvantages are: they are much more expensive to buy, more expensive to use (much more if run on batteries), and the large handles make them cumbersome to manipulate. An important additional disadvantage may be that people rely on them to find plaque, instead of looking for it themselves.

If you think your children will become more interested in tooth brushing with an electric toothbrush, it may be a worthwhile investment. If some member of your family has difficulty in moving his wrist, an electric toothbrush will be of benefit. Otherwise these brushes will have more of an impact on your pocket than your family's dental health.

WOODEN STICKS, TOOTHPICKS, AND GUM MASSAGERS

Toothpicks are designed to remove food caught between the teeth, and are not very good at removing plaque. Floss is better at both. One reason for this is that wooden toothpicks are usually round in cross section and fairly bulky, so they don't fit easily between the teeth. If food often catches between your teeth, especially fibrous food such as meat, the best answer is to see a dentist about it. The common reason is that a filling doesn't contact the next tooth properly, and this can and should be replaced.

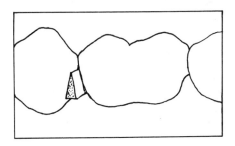

Fig. 24. Triangular wooden stick correctly placed.

Special wooden sticks with a **triangular** cross section are made (brand names include Sanodent and Interdens). These fit well between the teeth if there has been some gum recession in the area which you wish to clean. They are not useful for children who have had little gum recession, because there is not space for them to be inserted. They are easier to use than floss, though not quite so effective. The technique is to push the stick **gently** between two teeth, and move it backwards and forwards horizontally – not up and down like floss. The slightly rough surface of the wood will remove plaque from the two tooth surfaces. If you have a choice of wood hardness, buy the harder kind because the softer ones tend to break off and get stuck. I frequently recommend their use to elderly people who are less nimble with their hands and may have difficulty in mastering the use of floss. They also tend to have larger spaces between the necks of their teeth.

Some toothbrushes have small rubber spikes at the end of the handle, for massaging the gum. There is no evidence that massaging the gum has any beneficial effect, except that caused by the coincidental removal of plaque. The same applies to the triangular sticks, which are sometimes sold as 'Gum Massagers'. Their only value is in removing the plaque, at which they are a lot better than the rubber spikes.

WATER JETS

High pressure water jets, powered by little motors, are available for use at home. Though these are interesting and fun to use, and fairly good at dislodging pieces of food stuck to the teeth or in gum pockets, they are **very bad at removing plaque**, and a waste of money for that purpose.

TOOTHPASTE

Toothpaste has little effect on the removal of plaque, and therefore is not strictly necessary. Those of you who hate the taste will be pleased to hear this. However, I use it and will continue to, because I like the taste, and regard it as a present to myself for cleaning my teeth. My mouth feels fresher after I have cleaned my teeth with toothpaste.

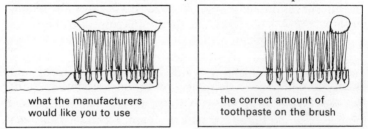

what the manufacturers would like you to use

the correct amount of toothpaste on the brush

Fig. 25. Correct amount of toothpaste on toothbrush.

There is another important point. Most toothpastes contain small amounts of fluoride, which have a significant decay-reducing effect – more than was at first thought. Recent evidence suggests that it may be as much as 30 per cent. So for your children's sake **use a fluoride toothpaste**. It will have less effect on adults' teeth which are already highly mineralized, but it will have some, and it will help adults avoid secondary decay around fillings as well as root decay.

Provided you pick a fluoride toothpaste, follow your own preference in price and flavour.

SMOKERS' TOOTH POWDERS AND PASTES

Ordinary powders and pastes have a low abrasive effect, but smokers' tooth powders contain more serious abrasives, intended to make it easier to brush off tobacco stains from the teeth. If these are used daily, there is a serious risk of wearing the teeth away, especially the dentine at the neck of the teeth. Therefore you should restrict your use of a smokers' powder or paste to specific occasions when you wish to remove stain. If only used once a week with a good toothbrush technique (not just scrubbing), the damage to the teeth would remain undetectable after many years. If used more often, or with bad technique, abrasion of the teeth might become visible. Abrasive powders and pastes can help remove any kind of stain, not only tobacco, and would work with the greenish stain which some young children produce in the plaque on their teeth (though of course if the plaque had been removed, this stain would not have occurred).

MOUTHWASHES

Many people believe that antiseptic mouthwashes are good for oral health. In fact most of them have little effect beyond that of giving your mouth a fresh feeling. The only mouthwash of proven value is chlorhexidine which I

101

mentioned before as being partially effective against plaque bacteria. However, because it leaves a yellow film on the teeth after prolonged use, you should only use it under the supervision of your dentist.

9

Strengthening teeth: fluoride and fissure sealants

Fluorine is an element which combines with certain other elements to form salts called **fluorides** (pronounced 'flue-or-rides' or just 'flue-rides'), and these salts are soluble in water to some degree. They are present in low concentrations in drinking water, concentrations which are usually expressed as 'parts per million' or **p.p.m.** A fluoride concentration of 1 p.p.m., for example, means that one gram of fluoride would be present in a million grams (1000 litres) of water. Of if, like me, you still think in ounces, one ounce of fluoride in over 6000 gallons.

It was noticed in America in the 1930s and soon after that in Britain, that children, who lived in areas where there was a higher than usual amount of fluoride naturally occurring in drinking water, had much less tooth decay than those living in low fluoride areas. The British story was an interesting one. During the war, a school dentist in the Newcastle area noticed a marked difference between the decay rates of children living in South Shields and those living close by in North Shields. These areas received different water supplies, and it was found on analysis that while North Shields had a low fluoride level, South Shields had a higher level which seemed to be associated with resistance to decay. This was subsequently proved when fluoride artificially added to water in many other parts of the world produced the same effect.

Further investigations showed that there was an optimum level of fluoride, 1–3 p.p.m., above or below which the decay resistance was less good. At this optimum fluoride level the reduction of decay rate was dramatic – **at least 50 per cent** – in other words only half the number of holes.

In some areas the naturally occurring fluoride levels are much higher – as high as 6 p.p.m. These high natural levels appear to have no effect at all on the general health of people drinking the water, but they have one unwanted effect on teeth. The decay rate remains low, but many of the teeth have small white or brown patches in the enamel, which spoil their appearance. In severe cases, there are even tiny pits in the enamel. These changes are technically called **mottling**. The relationship of decay and mottling with different fluoride concentrations in the water supply can best be shown by a graph.

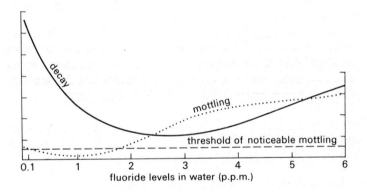

Fig. 26. How decay rate and mottling vary with water fluoride levels (temperate climates).

From this graph you can see that the lowest level of decay is around 2–3 p.p.m. but because mottling is socially unacceptable, **1 p.p.m. is taken as the ideal concentration in water** for water consumption in temperate climates. At that level there is also a considerable amount of decay prevention, about 80 per cent of the maximum possible by fluoride alone. In tropical areas where fluid consumption is greater, lower levels are recommended.

HOW DOES FLUORIDE WORK?

The effects of fluoride are two-stage. First, fluoride is absorbed into the body after being swallowed and is used by the tooth-forming cells to make crystals with minute quantities of fluoride built into them. These crystals are less soluble than the usual ones and resist acid attack better. Second, after the teeth erupt into the mouth, fluoride from drinking water and other sources in the diet is deposited directly onto the surface crystals of the enamel, and the material between the crystals, with an even greater reduction in solubility. In fact, the outer surface of the enamel has the highest concentrations of fluoride, over 500 p.p.m., about ten times the levels in the deeper layers. When acid is produced in the plaque film, crystals with fluoride in and around them stand up to it much better.

There are two other ways in which fluoride may help teeth: by taking part in remineralization of early decay sites (in areas with fluoridated water far more of the decay spots found on teeth are 'arrested'), and by inhibiting the activity of the plaque bacteria (bacteria don't like fluoride).

We can therefore divide the application of fluoride as a decay-preventing agent into two areas – fluoride you drink (or eat), and fluoride you put on the tooth surface.

FLUORIDE IN THE DIET

Water supplies vary in their natural fluoride content. Most of them have less than 1 p.p.m., a few have more. In a few areas in the UK and many in some other countries (the USA and the Republic of Ireland to name two), fluoride is added to the water to control decay.

Tea and fish are the only other dietary sources which contain significant quantities of fluoride. Tea made with water having negligible fluoride contains about 1.5 p.p.m. Fish has about 1 p.p.m. in its flesh, and higher levels in the skin and bones. If the level in water is low you can add fluoride to the diet as explained below.

FLUORIDE APPLIED TO THE TOOTH SURFACES: 'TOPICAL' FLUORIDE

This includes water, tea, etc., on their way to the stomach, fluoride toothpaste and fluoride rinses for home use, and strong fluoride preparations which the dentist can apply. In the past, the increased resistance to decay shown by many adults was probably due to dietary fluoride on its passage through the mouth. In future it will probably be attributed to fluoride toothpaste which began to be widespread in the early 1970s.

The dentist can obtain very strong fluoride solutions for application to the surfaces of the teeth. These are called 'topical' fluorides and should not be supplied for home use because they are not safe to have within reach of children. There is also one fluoride-containing varnish (Duraphat) which the dentist can paint on to the teeth and which falls off after a couple of days having given up a lot of its fluoride to the tooth surface, However, as I have said, the infrequent application of fluoride by the dentist is probably not nearly as effective as daily exposure to it at home, especially when combined with sugar control.

THE DANGERS OF FLUORIDE AND OBJECTIONS TO ITS USE

Fluoride is a poison, a point stressed by anti-fluoridation groups. But then so are table salt, water, oxygen, beer, aspirin, sugar, and so on. Yet they are used widely and some of them are indispensable for life. What makes the difference is **how much** of them you have. Oxygen, if breathed in too high concentration for too long, results in oxygen poisoning, as divers found in the First World War. If you drink too much water or eat too much salt you may seriously upset the balance of substances in the blood. Chronic alcohol poisoning is fairly common. Excess sugar leads to diabetes, artery disease, and heart failure, also common. Aspirin is used by a few people to kill themselves. If you eat enough fluoride you can also die. But the dose which will cause death is **several hundred times greater than that required to protect the teeth**, a much greater safety factor than that of alcohol or aspirin. For an average five-year-old child weighing 20 kg (44 lb) it would require 1000 of the strongest fluoride tablets to be fatal, and 60, or so, tablets to make him feel sick.

For children of four years and up, the daily requirement of fluoride to produce the best resistance to decay is 1 milligram (one thousandth of a gram). To help you visualize this, the amount of pure fluoride which could be picked up between finger and thumb, a pinch of salt, contains 120 times this. Three pinches would be a year's supply. Of course, you don't use pure fluoride – fluoride tablets or drops for children are very dilute. Later I shall explain in detail how you decide whether you need to give fluoride to your children and if so, how much. Here I am trying to convey the vast difference between a dose which could make you ill, and a dose which protects teeth. It is this difference which opponents of fluoride fail to distinguish.

The proof of its long-term safety rests with studies of people who grow up and live all their lives in areas with high levels of fluoride naturally occurring in their drinking water. In temperate climates people who drink water containing 6 p.p.m., and who are therefore taking in, every day, several times the optimum amount of fluoride, suffer only one disadvantage – mottling of the teeth. Nothing else. In addition, over 17 million people in the United States have now consumed fluoridated water for about twenty-five years with no adverse effects on health. The Food and Nutrition Board of the United States National Research Council has gone so far as to state that fluoride is an essential nutrient.

It may be that, in spite of my efforts to persuade you, the principle of giving a 'chemical' to your children is repellent to you. You should remember, though, that table salt is a chemical, too, and very similar to fluoride, and that sugar is also a chemical, as are vitamins. But, **if you just can't bear it, don't do it** even though you will be losing the decay-preventing effect, and your children will be more liable to get holes in their teeth. However, if you use fluoride toothpaste, and are very careful about sugar control, plaque removal, and taking your children for dental checks, although they may require some fillings rather than none, they oughtn't to **lose** any teeth. Some dentists' children haven't had fluoride tablets, and still don't get any decay. They haven't had many sweets either!

WHY IS THERE AN ANTI-FLUORIDATION LOBBY?

Artificial fluoridation of water supplies is a topic which is of exactly the right size to attract groups of people who are concerned with the romantic rather than the practical aspects of citizens' rights, pollution, ecology, etc. The idea of adding anything to natural water is repugnant to them. However, fluoride is present at some level in all water supplies and the 'natural' water we get through our taps is not really natural, because the water authorities must treat it to make it safe to drink. First they must add chlorine to the water to kill harmful bacteria, then ammonia or sulphur dioxide to convert the chlorine gas to soluble compounds, such as chloramines and salts. The water coming through most of our taps contains about 0.22 p.p.m. chlorine which is left over after the disinfection process. Without this treatment we would have many more cases of stomach upsets, and quite a few of cholera and typhoid. Some people would die from drinking tap water.

Now, any groups which protested against the treatment of water with chemicals to prevent diseases like cholera and typhoid would get little popular support. And any individual who demanded the right to have 'natural' untreated water, and take his chances with the bacteria, would make little headway, even if he pointed out what is absolutely true, that chlorine is an extremely poisonous chemical in high enough concentrations. Where it is a life and death issue; there is no argument, no controversy.

Tooth decay is not a life and death issue. Only a handful of people die even as the indirect result of it. But many people suffer inconvenience, social embarrassment, pain, and fear as a result of tooth decay and its effects. We are nowadays becoming increasingly interested in improving the quality of our lives, not just our survival. It seems to me that the quality of life and health must be improved by measures which reduce the incidence of tooth decay.

Of these, the simplest and most cost effective is the controlled fluoridation of those water supplies with less than 1 p.p.m. of naturally-occurring fluoride. Currently the costs of this would be about 15 pence per person per year in Britain, or 20 cents in the USA – very much less than the

"Look, let's start worrying about your moral objections to fluoride in the water supply if and when the occasion arises!"

Fig. 27.

cost of the dental treatment which it would prevent. As Ernest Newbrun points out in his excellent book[1] on tooth decay, 'In these days of rising health care costs, it is a rare bargain'. Fluoridation can do no harm (except temporarily, perhaps, to the incomes of dentists) and it is of lifelong benefit to young children whose teeth are developing. Adults also benefit, to a lesser extent, from its decay-reducing properties. In the USA 108 million people, nearly half the population, drink water which has been fluoridated. Australia also has large scale water fluoridation and so does New Zealand. In all, some 40 countries in the world, and 230 million people receive artificially-fluoridated water, and another 110 million drink water with naturally-occurring fluoride at levels which prevent decay.

So why does only 10 per cent of the population in the UK have similar protection?

There are several reasons for this. First, there is an anti-fluoridation lobby, which I have mentioned. Next, the dental profession in Britain is at fault, I believe, in having been very passive over the issue. Individual dentists are not used to lobbying or public debates, and they may feel that the benefits of fluoride are so obvious that it's up to the public to take action if they want to take action. (In the USA and Australia the fluoridation campaign was led by the dental profession – with the successes mentioned above.) Then there are administrative difficulties. Out of 90 Area Health Authorities in England and Wales, 87 voted to fluoridate the water supplies and all the major cities have said yes. But several different areas may receive water from a single source, and, if one of the areas does not agree, then none of them gets it. Much more important than this, however, is that Water Boards say that the legal position is not clear as to their right to fluoridate water. They are

[1]Newbrun, E. (1983) *Cariology* (2nd edn). Williams & Wilkins: Baltimore.

obliged to add things to water to make it 'wholesome', but the legal definition of the word is uncertain, and they do not regard as adequate the indemnity cover offered by central government against prosecutions brought by anti-fluoridationists. The word 'wholesome' must imply measures to prevent life-endangering diseases, but whether it would extend to other diseases, in particular dental decay, is not clear. What is really needed is a central government decision in favour of fluoridation, and a corresponding change in the law, but it is in this area that the anti-fluoridation lobby is so successful. However, there are hopeful signs. A recent and very thorough examination of the controversy in the Scottish courts (the Strathclyde case) has found that water fluoridation is quite safe, is positively beneficial to health and, paradoxically, illegal under Scottish law. The absurdity of this paradox may well accelerate the necessary facilitating legislation, but, in the meantime, it is up to individual households to add fluoride to the diet where necessary.

HOW TO DECIDE WHETHER YOU NEED TO USE FLUORIDE

The first thing you have to do is to find out how much fluoride there is in your mains water. You should be able to do this by looking at your local phone book under 'Water' to obtain the number of your local water authority (this number is also usually printed on the water bill). You then phone the local water office, or write to the Manager at that address and ask two questions:

(1) What is the fluoride level in the water I receive,

(2) does this level vary at different times of the year and if so, can you tell me the range, i.e. the highest and the lowest levels?

In answer to your first question you may receive the immediate response, 'We don't add fluoride to the water'. You must then repeat the question, 'Can you tell me the

natural fluoride level?' This should produce a straightforward answer expressed in parts per million (it will usually be less than 1, for example 0.3 p.p.m.).

The second question is necessary because water is supplied from a locally-interconnected system which may have various sources. With seasonal and local variations in rainfall, the water coming through your taps may come from different sources at different times, with varying fluoride levels. The only areas in which this variation would not occur, are those where fluoride is added artificially to bring it to the optimum 1 p.p.m., and the water is constantly being monitored for natural fluoride before any is added.

When you know the range of variation, take the highest level and look at the following table (mg means milligram, that is one thousandth of a gram. There are 28 grams in one ounce) to see how much fluoride your child should be taking each day.

For example, if you are told that the average level of fluoride is 0.2 p.p.m. and that it varies by 10 per cent up and down, the figure you should use is 0.22 p.p.m. This means

HOW MUCH FLUORIDE TO GIVE EACH DAY

Based[1] on recommendations of the American Dental Association (1979) and Dowell & Joyston-Bechal for the British Dental Association (1981)

Age of child	Maximum fluoride level in water		
	Less than 0.3 p.p.m.	0.3–0.7 p.p.m.	More than 0.7
0–6 months	None	None	None
6 months–2 years	¼ mg	None	None
2–4 years	½ mg	¼ mg	None
4–14 years	1 mg	½ mg	None

[1]The starting age for giving the first fluoride supplement is later in this table. The American dosage is from birth and the British from 2 weeks old, but it seems unlikely that fluoride in the first six months would make any real difference.

that you would give nothing before 6 months, ¼ mg every day to a child aged less than 2, ½ mg every day to a child aged 2–4 years, 1 mg every day to a child aged 4–14 years.

If the fluoride level in your water is above 0.7 p.p.m. do not give any additional fluoride. To do so might produce mottling of the teeth. But it's all right to use fluoride toothpaste in small quantities each time.

HOW TO GIVE FLUORIDE

Fluoride for home use is available in tablet form, in drops from a bottle, in mouth rinses, and in toothpastes. The first two are for swallowing.

Tablets	¼ mg each	
	½ mg each	For
	1 mg each	swallowing
Drops	⅛ mg per drop	
Mouth-rinses	0.05 per cent sodium fluoride (daily)	
	0.2 per cent sodium fluoride (weekly)	Not for
Toothpaste	½ inch contains 1 mg (but one brand,	swallowing
	Colgate, has recently increased its	
	fluoride level by 45 per cent)	

Tablets of all three concentrations and fluoride drops are available over the counter **without prescription** from many chemists (drug stores). They are quite cheap, a year's supply for one child costs about £2.50 (approximately US $3.75).

If you have found that your mains water fluoride level is less than 0.3 p.p.m. I suggest that you use the following daily regime for your children.

0–6 months	no fluoride
6 months–2 years	two fluoride drops per day placed directly in the mouth, changing to one ¼ mg tablet when the back teeth have come through
2 years–4 years	one ½ mg tablet placed inside the cheek and left there at bed time
4 years–14 years	one 1 mg tablet placed inside the cheek and left there at bed time.

The use of drops rather than tablets during the first phase of fluoride supplementation, is helpful because of limited co-operation by an infant. If you can't put them directly into the mouth, put them in a drink. From two years on, or whenever the back teeth come through, co-operation should be better. Changing to a tablet, which the child places inside the cheek after getting into bed (and if possible forgets is there) will provide a double benefit. First, the tablet slowly dissolves in the mouth, which bathes the first set of teeth in fluoride, and increases the remineralization of the tooth surfaces. Secondly, when it is swallowed the fluoride is absorbed into the second set of permanent teeth forming in the jaws. It is best to buy fluoride tablets with a fairly bland taste. Some brands have strong fruit flavours, no doubt to make them more acceptable to children, but these also stimulate the saliva flow, which washes the tablet away faster. Completely unflavoured tablets have little appeal, tasting rather chalky.

The best way to administer supplementary fluoride would be in divided doses, one in the morning and one in the evening. I hesitate to mention this because surveys have shown, not surprisingly, that even the chore of administering one fluoride tablet a day to a child becomes too much hassle for more than half the parents who start with good intentions. There are so many other things to worry about when you are bringing up children. Not having to remember is one of the advantages of water fluoridation. But since any reader of this book who has read this far is likely to be a more than average parent, and since some people really do want to know what is absolutely the best advice going at the time, here is the reason why a divided dose is recommended.

As I have said, the only danger from fluoride at the levels we are discussing is the risk of mottling, and mottling only starts to become a risk at **twice** the daily recommended dose. But what really matters is the level of fluoride in the blood at any one moment because it is this, if too high, which disturbs the enamel-producing cells and creates mottling. Water fluoridation is ideal because, as well as saving you the trouble of giving supplements, it produces very little impact on the blood fluoride level. Nobody drinks their complete daily fluid intake at one go. But when a five-year-old child takes a 1 mg tablet, she is getting most of the day's fluoride requirement at once, and the blood level can go up into the mottling range **if combined** with fluoride from toothpaste inadvertently swallowed. Provided you use the very small amount of fluoride toothpaste I suggest below (the 'small pea' size) then this risk is avoided and there can be no mottling. But some dentists recommend, to parents whom they think can cope, dividing the daily dose into two in order to produce lower 'peaks' of fluoride in the blood. At the age when your child, living in a very low fluoride area, qualifies (on turning four) for 1 mg of fluoride per day, you carry on using the ½ mg tablets you already have, but give one at breakfast, and the other, as before, at bedtime. If you live in an intermediate fluoride area (0.3–0.7 p.p.m.) there is no need to go to this trouble, because half the day's requirement is already in the water, so you can convert from the ¼ mg to the ½ mg bed time tablet on schedule.

Another detail for the fluoride connoisseur is that it is estimated that a typical cup of tea, made with low fluoride water, contains about 0.2 mg of fluoride – just less than a quarter of the daily fluoride requirement for a child of four and above. If your child happens to like tea, you might take that into account. Some teas have rather less fluoride than that, and the fluoride in tea from leaves topped up with a second lot of water is about half that strength. Any small amount of milk you may add will make little difference. (Any small amount of sugar you put in will make a very big difference.)

IMPORTANT – If you forget to give fluoride one day, DO NOT double the dose the next day.

You should just carry on as if you had not forgotten. Some dentists have found that their children developed mild mottling when double doses had been given. Similarly, it is quite wrong of one supplier of fluoride tablets to print on the label '½ tablet daily *or 1 every two days'* (my italics).

Toothpaste swallowing

Many people assume, not without help from the toothpaste manufacturers, that the entire length of the toothbrush bristles should be spread with the full thickness of toothpaste out of the tube. But this half-inch of toothpaste (about 1 g) contains the **daily** dose of fluoride for a four-year-old child, and would probably be used twice a day. Studies have shown that, when that much toothpaste is used, the pre-school child, not always able to spit out completely, may swallow 0.3–0.4 g of the toothpaste, that is 30–40 per cent of the daily fluoride dose, at each brushing. This amount, when added to the correct dietary fluoride intake, whether in the water supply or in the home supplements, would bring the total daily dose up to a level where there was a risk of mottling.

Later on, children become more efficient at rinsing and spitting out, but in any case there is no justification for using as much toothpaste as the advertisers, with their pictures of heavily-laden toothbrushes, would like. A much better idea for all the family is to use a very small amount of toothpaste on the end of the brush – this is generally expressed as 'the size of a small pea'. Even if most of this were swallowed, it would make little difference to the daily dose of fluoride. In addition, your toothpaste bill will drop dramatically. A large tube of toothpaste should last one person for a year.

Occasionally, young children intentionally eat toothpaste from the tube, because they like the taste. If you suspect this has happened, don't give the fluoride supplement that day, and move the tube to some safe place.

IS THERE ANY ADVANTAGE TO A CHILD FROM A MOTHER'S TAKING FLUORIDE SUPPLEMENTS BEFORE THE CHILD IS BORN?

It used to be thought that the placenta blocked the passage of fluoride to the unborn baby. This is now doubted. Improved analysis techniques have shown that new-born babies have fluoride levels in the blood only slightly lower than those of their mothers. Nevertheless, the question of whether raising the prenatal fluoride levels in the mother confers any subsequent benefit on the child is still controversial. Some reports suggest that taking fluoride when you are pregnant does help, but others indicate that it doesn't. In many of these studies the experimental or statistical method left something to be desired.

Because of this uncertainty, and because in any case only the tips of some of the baby teeth have mineralized by the time the baby is born, the current concensus view is that prenatal fluoride supplements provide so little advantage that they are not worth taking. Indeed, as you will see from the table on page 112, I do not even consider they are worth giving to the baby until it is six months old, in the lowest fluoride areas. (The equivalent official recommendation is 'from birth' in the USA and 'from two weeks old' in the UK).

FLUORIDE AND ADULTS

Fluoride does benefit adults, but less than it benefits children. Adults' teeth have already formed, erupted, and had surface mineralization. Dietary fluoride, on its rapid passage through the mouth may contribute a little more than fluoride tablets. Adults with unusually high decay rates can benefit from strong fluoride rinses provided by a dentist. Fluoride toothpaste may also increase mineralization and reduce sensitivity of the necks of the teeth.

A final comment on fluoride: A study has shown that where dietary fluoride (where the water is fluoridated) is the **only**

anti-decay measure being used, but children don't get their teeth cleaned and do eat significant amounts of sugar, a small number of five-year-olds (about 4 per cent) still have rapid decay. The point is that fluoride on its own is not a complete protection. The other measures are necessary as well if you want no decay.

FISSURE SEALANTS

You may remember that, in describing the shape of teeth, I said there was one area of tooth surface which neither floss nor the brush could reach, and which therefore could not be cleaned of plaque. This is the fissure, or crevice, which is part of the biting surface of the back teeth. To deal with this problem, special watertight **varnishes** have been developed which block up the bottom of the fissure and prevent plaque from forming there. In other words they seal the fissures against acid attack and are called, sensibly enough, fissure sealants.

These have to be applied by the dentist, because the tooth surface must be prepared so that the varnish will bond to it. The dentist first cleans the tooth carefully, then applies a special acid solution to the fissure surface, to 'etch' it. This sounds like a mad thing to do when we know that it is acid which causes decay, but actually the effect is more like that of lemon juice, which dissolves some of the surface crystals and makes the surface rough on a microscopic scale. This roughness is what allows the varnish to lock on to the surface of the enamel by flowing all around the crystals. When it sets, it cannot be lifted off and forms an imperme-able barrier against any further acid attack. It must be done **very carefully**, because once the enamel surface has been etched, washed to remove the acid and dried, absolutely no saliva must be allowed to get on to the tooth surface before the varnish, or else the varnish will not penetrate the microscopic spaces between the crystals and will not form a good mechanical bond. For this reason the most careful dentists use a sheet of rubber called a **rubber dam** to separate the crown of the tooth from the rest of the mouth, and it takes some time to do properly, sometimes as long as a filling. So the dentist needs to have a relaxed and co-operative child. But once the sealant is in place, it is unlikely that there will ever be any decay in the fissure.

The advantages of fissure sealants are that the technique is peaceful and painless, that it avoids the need for fillings in that part of the tooth, and that the teeth remain healthy and strong. Fissure sealants have only been around for about fifteen years, so we do not know for sure that they will last indefinitely, but providing they are properly applied we cannot see any reason why they won't. They certainly last for the period of principal decay risk. The more recent products are not clear varnishes, but contain tooth-coloured particles. This makes them easier to check and probably more resistant to wear.

The time to start thinking about asking a dentist to apply fissure sealant is when your child is about 5½ years old. This is when you want to start looking for the first permanent molars which come into the mouth immediately behind the last baby teeth top and bottom. Baby teeth are not usually treated with sealant, but these four first permanent teeth are very important and very prone to decay. When all four have emerged in the mouth, make tracks to the dentist and ask about getting them sealed. It is in the early months that they are most vulnerable to attack before they have built up their level of surface mineralization. The second set of molars make their appearance about the age of twelve and can be similarly treated. Not all dentists use sealants with their own children because experience has shown that with fluoride, sugar control, and good cleaning, even the fissures are unlikely to decay. Some dentists don't use sealants at all, and some who do reserve them for children who are known to be prone to decay.

SUMMARY ON FLUORIDE AND FISSURE SEALANTS

1. Fluoride occurs naturally in water in low concentrations and is totally safe for general health up to 6 p.p.m. (most natural water supplies have less than 1 p.p.m. fluoride). In areas where the fluoride concentration is below a recommended level, fluoride supplements are advised.

2. Fluoride protects the teeth against decay by making tooth crystals more resistant to acid attack.

3. It is absorbed into these crystals (a) before the teeth erupt by being swallowed and reaching the tooth forming cells (**dietary fluoride**), (b) after the teeth erupt, by being absorbed directly into the crystals of the surface layer of the enamel (**topical fluoride**) where it is most useful.

4. The ideal level of fluoride in drinking water in temperate climates is 1 part per million (1 p.p.m.). In tropical areas, where people drink more because of the heat, a lower level is preferred.

5. In areas where the natural fluoride level is higher, no harm occurs to general health, but small white or brown patches may be present on the enamel of the teeth (mottling), and above 4 p.p.m. the resistance to decay decreases.

6. The protection which fluoride can give is at least 50 per cent – that is children would have only half the number of holes. If that is added to other measures recommended in this book they should have **no dental decay at all**, in other words, perfect teeth. This is what happens with many dentists' children.

7. You can find out how much fluoride you have in your drinking water by asking your local water authority (see phone book or water bill). The level may vary a little during the year.

8. If the highest level is above 0.7 p.p.m. you should not add fluoride to the diet of your children. They will be

getting good protection. If it is 0.7 p.p.m. or less, giving additional fluoride every day will help their teeth.

9. Once you have found out your local fluoride level, consult the table in this chapter to see how much you should provide for your children at different ages. If your water authority tells you that it has decided to add fluoride to the water to bring it to over 0.7 p.p.m., stop giving dietary fluoride from the specified date. You can continue to use fluoride toothpaste.

10. If you forget to give fluoride one day **do not** give extra the next day.

11. Develop in your child the habit of using only a very small amount of toothpaste each time (the size of a pea or less). The manufacturers recommend more for obvious reasons. And watch out for signs of secret toothpaste eating (not very common). If so, put the toothpaste in a safe place.

12. Fissure sealants block up the only part of the tooth surface which cannot be cleaned by anything, and which are therefore prone to decay – the fissures of the back teeth.

13. Fissure sealants must be applied carefully by the dentist, and are best put on as soon as the permanent back teeth erupt enough to be properly isolated from saliva. The first permanent molars come through from about the age of 5½.

Questions on fluoride and fissure sealants (answers on pages 148 and 149)

1. Can fluoride ever be dangerous?
2. Can your dentist fluoridate your teeth for you?
3. What advantage is there in letting fluoride tablets dissolve in the mouth?
4. If you are giving fluoride supplements to your child, does it matter if he eats toothpaste?

10

Plaque and gum disease

In the subtitle of this book I promised to tell you how to save your own teeth as well as your children's. And in Chapter 2 I said that, over a lifetime, gum disease is likely to cause more tooth loss than decay, and that it comes into prominence during your thirties, by which time some considerable damage may have been done.

WHAT IS GUM DISEASE?

Gum disease is a chemically complicated but conceptually simple process of inflammation of the gums. It is caused by plaque, and without plaque there is no gum disease. This means, in effect, that I have already told you how to cure it: just remove all the plaque from your teeth often enough (as described in Chapter 7).

If you decide not to do this (and it is absolutely your right **not** to clean your teeth effectively – as Rod Steiger said in a film about something else, 'It doesn't mean you're a bad person'!), then you will almost certainly continue to have progressive gum disease, and the following things will be going on:

First Stage

The plaque lying on the teeth next to the gums causes them to become:
red (rather than pale pink)
slightly swollen (rounded and shiny rather than thin and stippled like orange peel)

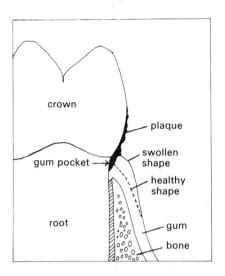

Fig. 28. Early stage of gingivitis.

liable to bleed when brushed (because of tiny ulcers in the gum pocket)

There is no pain

Appearance: All of these changes you can see for yourself by looking in a mirror

Treatment: These changes can be reversed, and the gum made healthy simply by removing plaque completely every day. To make this possible it may be necessary to have your teeth smoothed by a dentist.

Second stage

After some months or years of this inflammation, the plaque lying on the teeth will cause the uppermost fibres between root and bone to rot, and this will be followed by the loss of the bone to which they were attached. The gum pocket will also become deeper as the bone level falls. The gum remains red, swollen, and liable to bleed when brushed. Still no pain.

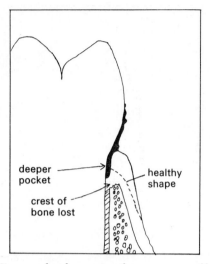

Fig. 29. Gum pocket becoming deeper – start of bone loss.

Appearance: The situation looks the same as before to you but a dentist can measure the pockets and find that they have become deeper (more than 2 mm).
Treatment: Removing the plaque every day will make the gums perfectly healthy again, although you won't regain the lost bone, and the gum should shrink to a new healthy shape slightly lower on the tooth.

Third stage

After many years without good plaque removal you will reach the third stage. By now a lot of bone has been lost and the gum has shrunk down, but not so fast as the bone. The gum pocket has therefore become much deeper (more than 6 mm). Because of the bone loss, the tooth may start to feel a little loose, and front teeth sometimes start to drift. Redness, swelling, and bleeding as before. Still no pain.

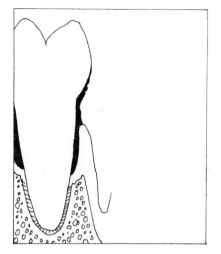

Fig. 30. Less than half the root still in bone.

Appearance: Now you are noticeably long in the tooth (or else have very deep pockets).
Treatment: Removing the plaque every day is still the first step to retrieving the situation, **but you should now be under the active care of a dentist who can provide special gum treatment and supervise you.**

Final stage (not usually till your 40s or 50s but sometimes sooner).

After some more years without good plaque removal and gum treatment the last stage is reached. Most of the bone has, by now, been lost around many of the teeth so some of them are very loose and **starting to hurt**. This takes you to the dentist, and he suggests that the worst of them (or perhaps all of them) should be taken out, because they are past saving, and dentures are made. You, in pain, and probably getting a bad taste in the mouth are only too happy to agree. Though you may not like the idea of dentures, they seem the lesser of two evils.

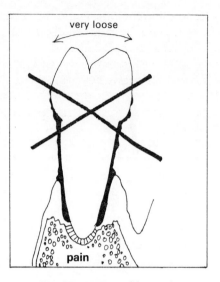

Fig. 31. Unsaveable tooth.

Result: You have joined the majority in losing your teeth because of gum disease.

The above sequence of events is common, but it does not have to happen if you start to remove plaque properly before it is too late. It certainly should not be allowed to happen to your children. They should be able to reap the benefit of being born at a time when we know how to prevent gum disease as well as decay.

CONCLUSION

To finish this chapter, instead of a summary I shall remind you of two points, the first from Chapter 6, and the second just mentioned.

It is very important that your teeth should be smooth if you are to remove plaque easily. This means that you must go to a dentist to have calculus removed and especially any overhangs (ledges) or roughness of imperfect fillings. You can tell you have these because the floss will fray when you remove it from between two teeth.

If you have advanced gum disease (stages three or four) it is best to take your gums to a dentist so that you can co-operate with him in saving the teeth. If you are going for a routine check, ask him to examine the gums anyway.

11

Does losing teeth matter?

As I said before, teeth are not the most important thing in most people's lives. For many of us they occasionally become critical – severe toothache drives almost everything else from the mind. But generally there are more pressing matters to occupy us in our daily lives. Losing front teeth may send us hurrying to the dentist to get replacements so that we can look normal. Losing back teeth is accepted with resignation as a fairly natural event. Even people who have no teeth left at all seem to manage reasonably well with complete dentures, though they tend to find the idea of them embarrassing. So does it really matter, and is it worth all the effort and attention needed to keep you teeth?

To answer this let us consider the proposition that it might be best to remove all the teeth, healthy or not, when people were twenty-one and give them nice sets of dentures. In certain parts of England this used to be done when a girl was going to be married, as part of her dowry. The idea was that it would save dental expense and inconvenience for the rest of her life. And probably for some of them it did.

But not everybody has an easy time with dentures. Biological variability strikes again.

THE EFFECTS OF LOSING ALL YOUR TEETH

When permanent teeth are removed, the bone that was around the roots disappears fairly quickly, say within the first six months. After that the bone continues to disappear in those areas, at a slower rate. This rate varies a great deal between different people. Some people who have had all their teeth out have big bony ridges, where their teeth were, years or even decades after the extractions. But others lose this bone very much faster. The bony ridges are important because they are what the dentures sit on, and what help to hold the dentures still in the mouth. The unfortunate people who lose bone rapidly, and they will continue to lose it as long as they live, reach the stage where it is very difficult to keep their dentures steady at all.

They move about when eating, and because of this, denture wearers avoid certain kinds of food which are more difficult to chew, or which become stuck under the dentures and hurt. Chewing **any** solid food may hurt because the soft gum over the shrunken ridges becomes squashed between the denture and the bone. Talking may be difficult because the dentures move, or because they are not exactly the right shape. There is the awful danger of the dentures dropping down in company. A few very socially sensitive people are so alarmed at this possibility that they become more or less housebound and don't welcome visitors.

I do not wish to exaggerate the prevalence of these problems. Remember, a great many people who have complete dentures get on with them satisfactorily (though few of them think they are as good as their own teeth). The difficulty is that we have no way of telling in advance if **you** will be a fast bone loser or a slow bone loser.

Another difference between people is their adaptability to having these foreign objects in their mouths. Some people are very good at wearing dentures, some very bad, and the majority in the middle. However, not everybody who jumps in the deep end (by losing all his teeth) knows whether he can swim. And a dentist can give no guarantees.

So, faced with these uncertainties, the good dentist becomes a professional pessimist and assumes the worst – that his patient will lose bone faster than average and will have a poorer than average ability to adapt to wearing dentures. If he adds to that the fact that not even the best denture is as strong as the natural teeth, can bite so hard, or is so well fixed to the jaws, it is no wonder that the good dentist tries to save teeth rather than remove them. Of course, in the end, if his patient doesn't do the homework, he may not succeed.

The time factor also plays a part in this discussion of the pros and cons of having complete dentures. If you lose all your teeth at the age of twenty-one and you live to be seventy-five, you will have fifty-four years of bone loss in your jaws. Even if you only have a moderate rate of bone loss, a great deal will have disappeared by your sixties. The dental hospitals, which deal with some of the more serious denture problems, have long waiting lists of elderly people whose **quality of life** has been reduced by their increasing difficulty in wearing dentures. They may have had several decades of success, but now things are getting really difficult, or they may never have had any success. There are many sad stories, specially sad because there is often not much to be done, once the bone has gone.

Bearing in mind the idea of biological variability, if you know some elderly people who are perfectly happy with dentures they have had for thirty years, don't let that persuade you that everyone else, especially you and your children, would be so lucky. You might be and you might not be. Knowing some ninety-year-old man who smokes fifty cigarettes a day, doesn't protect **you** from the effects of smoking.

LOSING SOME BUT NOT ALL YOUR TEETH

So far I have talked about what can happen if you, or your children, lose all your teeth. What about just losing some? The effects vary considerably with how many teeth and which teeth.

Let us start with **baby teeth**. Many people reason that losing baby teeth early through decay is not important, because they are going to be lost anyway. This isn't true, for several reasons:

1. Children like to look good, and to avoid the social

stigma and unkind remarks of other children, which having a 'gappy' smile may cause. You also will want your child to look attractive, have sweet breath, and so on, and not to have a difficult time at school.

2. In losing baby teeth from decay, the child will have been introduced to the dentist in the worst, most traumatic way, that of having extractions probably preceded by the miseries of toothache. The teeth will start to be associated in his mind with pain and tribulation, and the dentist to become an object of fear. **If you really want to guarantee a bad dental future for your child, all you have to do is to make sure he is afraid of the dentist.**

3. The reasons for losing baby teeth, too much sugar and too much plaque, are likely to continue with the permanent teeth. The 'sweet tooth' problem will have been created, and the child will have become used to that 'furry' feeling which plaque on the teeth gives.

4. The baby back teeth have a space-maintaining function. Normally the permanent first molar teeth, the biggest teeth of all, come through into the mouth behind the last (furthest back) of the baby teeth at about the age of six years. This is their correct position. If the baby back teeth are lost much before their natural time of falling out, those big molars tend to erupt, or even to drift, too far forward in the mouth. This leaves too little space for the front teeth, which then come through crowded in the front of the mouth. They grow down 'higglety-pigglety' and out of line. They look less attractive, and are more difficult to clean. It doesn't always happen, but it happens often enough to make it a good idea for baby teeth to fall out at the natural time, fairly painlessly, rather than early.

Losing **permanent teeth** can also cause problems. Drifting or tilting of the teeth either side into the gap happens quite often. This allows food to pack in between those teeth and their neighbours, which is uncomfortable and bad for the gums. In a minority of cases, the altered tooth position causes an altered way of biting which makes the jaw muscles go into painful spasms leading to headaches, clicking jaw joints, limited opening, etc. Teeth from the opposite jaw may grow down into the gap and limit chewing movements. There is obviously the problem of appearance where the gaps are visible. If you lose enough of the back teeth, you cannot chew so well, and, if you lose all of them, the front teeth, which now have to do all the chewing, start to wear down and may look too short. One could go on with a long list.

I must make the point again, that it is rare for all of these things to happen, and sometimes none of them happen, but **you can't tell in advance** which of them will or won't happen in any individual who loses teeth.

It isn't always a bad thing to lose some teeth. For example, orthodontists sometimes remove quite healthy teeth to give themselves space to straighten out crowded front teeth. Sometimes wisdom teeth for which there is no room in the mouth, or which are badly positioned in the jaw bone, are removed before, rather than after, they give trouble. Sometimes the dentist has tried everything he can think of to save a tooth, but it hasn't worked, the disease process around a root is continuing, and he and the patient agree that the tooth should come out. There are even a few serious illnesses where the patient's health may be at risk by keeping any teeth, and they are all removed. But these are usually teeth which already have a doubtful future because of gum disease.

Summing up, it seems to me that the argument for natural teeth in preference to artificial ones has been made very strongly. If you don't agree in your own case, that is your affair, and good luck to you. It is very important to realize that you have a total right to decide what you want for your own teeth. But you must think very carefully before you make a similar decision against natural teeth for your children.

I have said very little about the role of the dentist in saving teeth. Indeed, the principal aim of this book has been to reduce the amount of dental treatment needed by you and your family. But only the dentist can tell you that you do not need treatment, because only the dentist can carry out the necessary detailed examination and diagnosis.

12

Going to the dentist

Becoming the regular patient of a dentist you trust is essential to dental health,[1] but, as I said earlier, what you and your children do to protect your teeth is more important than anything the dentist can do. This is true for preventing gum disease and tooth decay and I stress the point because many people think, if they go to the dentist regularly, that is all that is necessary.

Once damage has occurred, however, it needs a dentist to put it right. And it usually needs a dentist to discover the damage in its early stages. I think it will save time if I list some of the things which dentists can do better than their patients:

1. Find decay (examination and X-rays).
2. Measure the extent of gum disease (for example, the depth of pockets and X-rays).
3. Remove calculus from teeth to make them smooth (scaling) and remove the ledges from bad fillings, crowns, etc. (I realize a dentist also created these!)
4. Provide fillings, crowns, bridges, and dentures to restore or replace damaged teeth.
5. Save roots of teeth by root fillings (endodontics).
6. Remove unwanted or unsaveable teeth (extractions).
7. Anticipate, measure, and treat poor positioning of teeth leading to unattractive appearance, reduced chewing efficiency and difficult cleaning (orthodontics).
8. Carry out surgery to deal with advanced gum disease and other conditions of the jaws.

[1] How to find a dentist in the UK is covered well by an article in *Which!* magazine ('Dentists', November 1979 pp.641–44).

9. Reassure patients that there is no need for anxiety over slight abnormalities in their mouths or that the problem can be dealt with.
10. Detect early signs of some general illnesses.
11. Guide people in their efforts at dental home-work (cleaning, diet, etc.).
12. Stop dental pain.

HOW OFTEN TO GO TO THE DENTIST, AND WHEN TO START

It is a good idea to introduce your child to the dentist at an early stage, when all the baby teeth have come through, but before anything has gone wrong. Age three is a suitable time. The dentist can talk to the child, have a game with the up and down chair and demonstrate that the dental surgery can be fun. A quick look in the mouth and praise for the nice teeth is a happy introduction to 'going to the dentist'.

Even this brief inspection will enable the dentist to decide how often he needs to see your child. Some young children may require four-monthly check-ups. Schoolchildren may be checked every six months, and adults (whose teeth have become more resistant to decay) often only need to have an examination, with perhaps a scaling, once a year or at longer intervals if their sugar control and oral hygiene is good.

ORTHODONTIC CHECKS

Most of this book has been concerned with stopping the ravages of tooth decay and gum disease. In many parts of the world the rates of tooth decay are already falling, along with sugar consumption. It seems probable that as the mere survival of children's teeth becomes a less pressing issue, and the time spent by dentists on repair work reduces, the opportunity will be created for parents and dentists alike to turn their attention to the positions and appearance of children's teeth. This has already happened in the USA.

If the resources existed for it, the ideal would be for all children to have an orthodontic assessment at the age of eight to ten years. The majority of children would be found to have teeth in satisfactory alignment, but quite a few, perhaps as many as 40 per cent, would be diagnosed as likely to benefit from eventual orthodontic treatment. In most cases treatment could be deferred until most of the permanent teeth have appeared in the mouth, which usually occurs by age eleven. In a few cases a short course of so-called 'interceptive orthodontic treatment' would be recommended at an earlier age.

The simpler forms of orthodontics can be carried out by the family dentist using removable appliances (braces), which can be taken out of the mouth for cleaning. Typically this involves one year of active tooth movement, followed by three to six months wearing a removable retainer to stop the teeth drifting back towards their original positions. Since many orthodontic problems are caused by crowding of the teeth in jaws which are too small for them, it is sometimes necessary to remove healthy teeth, usually one in each quarter of the mouth, to create the space necessary for the remainder. Occasionally this will even eliminate the need for further orthodontic treatment. For more complex cases, in which teeth have to be moved bodily through the jaw bone rather than just tipped gently into position, it is necessary to have the fine wires which produce the movement fixed to the teeth. This type of treatment is usually carried out, after referral from your own dentist, by a full-time specialist orthodontist. Active treatment with these 'fixed appliances' normally takes about 18 months, followed by a six months or longer retention period with a removable appliance which, in the later stages, is worn only at night. In both types of treatment the child usually visits the dentist once a month for adjustments.

In areas where orthodontic treatment is less common, a little persuasion of the child to accept treatment is sometimes required, because not all children are able to balance the life-long advantages of a beautiful smile and improved function against the short-term disadvantages of having wires on their teeth when most of their school friends don't. (The converse can also be true. I have heard of some children in the United States who feel deprived if they don't need orthodontic treatment!).

Some other points on tooth position:

- Thumb or finger-sucking may have an adverse effect on tooth position and if your child can be gently dissuaded from it, without generating emotional turbulence, that is a good idea.
- If either parent has badly aligned teeth, or used to have, there is an increased risk that the children also will.
- Bad tooth position is not just a matter of appearance. Prominent front teeth are more likely to get broken in sporting, playing or car accidents.
- Crowded teeth are more prone to decay and gum troubles because of the difficulty in cleaning them, and teeth which do not bite together well may give rise to jaw joint and muscle problems later in life.
- Baby teeth rarely need orthodontic treatment. It would have to be done all over again with the permanent teeth, anyway.
- Adults can have orthodontic treatment, but it usually takes a little longer because the bone around the teeth takes longer to remodel.

ACCIDENTS TO TEETH

While you are carefully superintending the development of healthy teeth and gums in your children, it would be a great pity if some of these perfect teeth got broken or even knocked out by a blow to the mouth. This is quite a common event.

Apart from obvious things like the use of seat belts or special seats in cars, and making sure that the children are sitting, not standing, when the car is in motion, there are other activities frequently associated with front tooth damage. I have had the embarrassment of being with a friend's daughter in a 'dodgem car' at a fun fair when she broke a tooth against the steering wheel, and bicycling, playing games, rushing around in the school playground, and especially team sports, may cause dental casualties. The hard edge of a swimming pool has also claimed a good few healthy teeth.

To avoid this risk, children's dentists are increasingly recommending the use of mouth guards to protect the teeth. Self-fitted versions may be bought in some shops, but the best are accurately fitting ones made by the dentist. They are thin, slightly flexible and cover the upper teeth and gums. The idea is that the force of a blow to the front teeth is dissipated via the other teeth in that jaw. Children with prominent front teeth are especially at risk because there is less protection from the lips.

If a tooth is actually knocked out and you can find it, there is a series of actions you can take. In order of reducing successfulness they are:

1. Wash the tooth quickly under **cold water** and put it quickly back in the socket, taking care to put it in the right way round. Doing this won't hurt. This is the best course of action and the faster it goes back the better the chances. Then go to the dentist at the earliest opportunity, where the tooth will be secured while healing takes place.

2. If neither you nor the child can bring yourself to do this, wash the tooth quickly in cold water and put it in a clean, cool, damp handkerchief and get to a dentist as fast as possible. (If it's 8 o'clock on a Friday night you may **have** to revert to the first method.) If the child is old enough to be relied upon, an even better vehicle for carrying the tooth is the child's own mouth – saliva

keeps the tooth at the best temperature and contains anti-infective agents.

DO NOT
- wash the tooth in hot water
- scrape the root clean
- dip the tooth in disinfectant
- let it dry out.

Following the reimplantation of a tooth, root treatment may be needed at a later stage, and an artificial crown may be required eventually. But at least there is a good chance that the all important root will have been saved. Filling a gap without the root is more difficult and sometimes less successful.

FEAR AND THE DENTIST

Nowadays dentistry can be carried out virtually painlessly because of high-speed drills and very good injection fluids. But, the tradition of pain and the accompanying fear lives on. It may be that you are really afraid of the dentist. And, if so, the chances are that your children will feel that fear, however much you may try to conceal it. Children are surprisingly sensitive to such things. If you are afraid, you might consider asking another member of the family, or a friend, to take your child to the dentist. And I should repeat the point that it is most undesirable for anybody's first experience of the dentist to be in connection with having teeth out.

CONCLUSION

Now that you have read this book and learnt something about the causes of dental disease and how to prevent it, you will be in a position to make a significant change in the dental future of your family.

Do not imagine that an informed patient is regarded by

the dentist as a threat. Dentists are most proud of their patients who no longer require treatment apart from an occasional scaling. This makes them optimistic about dental health. And dealing with people who are trying to **keep** their teeth is so much easier, and more pleasant, than doing filling after filling in mouths that are going downhill.

Part 2

Information package

A. Further reading

GENERAL READING

Cook, Richard and Elizabeth (1983). *Sugar Off!* Great Ouse Press, Cambridge.
Available from: Great Ouse Press, c/o B.S.U. Ltd, 43–45 Hobson Street, Cambridge CB1 1NL, England. Tel: Cambridge (0223) 521030. Price £3·95 (150 pages) including post & packing.
From 1985 a revised edition will be published by Pan Books.

PROFESSIONAL READING

Newbrun, Ernest (1983). *Cariology* (2nd edn). Williams and Wilkins, Baltimore and London.
Murray, J.J. and Rugg-Gunn, A.J. (1982). *Fluorides in caries prevention*. Wright PSG, Bristol and Boston.
Imfeld, T.N. (1983). *Identification of low caries risk dietary components*. (Monographs in Oral Science Vol.11). Karger, Basel.
Grenby, T.H. ed. (1983). *Development in sweeteners – 2*. Applied Science Publishers. London and New York.
James, W.P.T, chairman (1983). Proposals for nutritional guidelines for health education in Britain, prepared for the National Advisory Committee on Nutrition Education, and available, on written application, from the Health Education Council, 78 New Oxford Street, London WC1A 1AH (ask for the NACNE Report).

B. Answers to questions

CHAPTER 4 – PLAQUE, SUGAR, AND TOOTH DECAY

1. Is it better to clean your teeth before or after a meal?

Surprisingly, it is better to clean your teeth before a meal, if you do it really well. The reason is simply that if the plaque has been removed from the teeth before eating, any sugar in the food will remain as sugar, because there aren't any bacteria on the tooth surface to turn it into acid. That argument applies to decay prevention, but from the point of view of the gums it doesn't matter which side of a meal you clean your teeth. Remember the point of flossing and brushing is to remove plaque, not food.

There is a problem with this idea which I haven't touched upon. The flavour of toothpaste may not combine well with the meal which follows cleaning. What we really need is a special pre-prandial toothpaste with minimal flavouring, and these don't exist. One way out of this difficulty would be to clean your teeth carefully **without** toothpaste before eating and use a fluoride rinse after the meal (so that you don't damage the temporarily delicate surface crystals with a toothbrush). I realize that this suggestion adds to the general inconvenience of tooth care but it might recommend itself to people who are very sensitive to the conflict of taste.

2. Can you get decay from a meal which does not contain any foods with sugar in them?

The evidence is that you can't. You can get demineralization over large areas with the juice of lemons and other citrus fruit, but decay requires sugars and plaque.

3. **Is is possible to eat sugary foods without getting decay?**

Yes, in any of the following situations:

(a) If you have just previously removed **all** the plaque (see 1. above)

(b) If you are a person with a naturally high degree of resistance to decay and don't have sugar too often

(c) If your teeth have been made more insoluble by secondary mineralization with the passing of years (or actively by applying fluorides and fissure sealant – see Chapter 9)

(d) If you have no teeth left.

4. **Are yellowish teeth more or less resistant to decay than white teeth?**

This sounds like an old wives' tale, but generally speaking they **are** more resistant, providing we are talking about the real colour of the teeth and not some stain which has collected on the surface. The reason for this is that yellower teeth have more translucent enamel which allows the yellow of the dentine to show through more. This greater translucency is caused by a more mineralized enamel, which is therefore more resistant to decay.

Exception – If children whose teeth are developing are given the antibiotic **tetracycline**, their teeth may be made permanently greyish yellow without necessarily being resistant to decay. So this is a good drug to avoid during the first twelve years of life where there is an alternative. The literature on tetracyclines now carries this warning but some doctors are not aware of it, so it is worth querying a prescription for antibiotics on this point.

5. **Why do teeth decay less as you get older?**

a) Because, with time, minerals from food and drink

build up in the tooth surface and make it more insoluble.

b) Because many of the prime sites for decay may already have been filled by the dentist (my dentist told me to stop using toothpaste and start using metal polish!).

But beware! Even if you have not needed fillings for years, a return to frequent sweet snacks could leave you with a lot of new cavities. Adults sucking peppermints to help giving up smoking and pregnant mothers on sugar binges are some of the casualties.

CHAPTER 5 – SUGAR

1. **Why is it better for children to have sweets at meal times than between meals?**

Because the amount of decay depends on the number of times you have sugar every day. If the meal has contained sugar, and with our typical Western diet many meals do, then to have more sugar at about the same time will not produce a separate bout of acid production. Of course, it is still better not to have sweets at the end of meals (see next question). One interesting piece of research has shown that if you finish a meal with a piece of cheese, the acid level at the tooth surface is less. The reason for this may be that cheese stimulates the flow of saliva, and this may wash away sugar left in the mouth.

2. **If a meal contains sugar anyway, does it make any difference to have sweets as well at the end of the meal?**

Yes it does, for two reasons: (a) the contact of sugar with plaque is prolonged by the sweets which may produce a lower pH and therefore faster acid attack; (b) the presence of high concentrations of sugar normally contained in sweets encourages plaque build-up, both in the number of bacteria and the amount of glucan glue.

But if sweets are to be eaten at all, at the end of a **sugar-containing** meal is the proper place for them.

3. **Are natural foods containing sugar, such as honey, less decay-producing than synthetic foods to which sugar has been added?**

No, not really. If there is any difference, it is very slight. Honey is a very concentrated sugar solution with no other nutritional value. If it is true that sucrose is slightly worse for teeth than other sugars, then honey is slightly better because it does not contain sucrose. The types of natural sugar in fresh fruit are similar to those in honey, but at a much lower concentration, and therefore significantly safer. Another advantage of fruit is that with many hard fruits (e.g., apples and pears), if pieces are swallowed, a lot of the sugar is inside the pieces, and does not become released until they get past the mouth.

4. **Place the following foods in increasing order of decay production – cheddar cheese, cola drinks, drinks with less than one calorie per can/bottle, boiled sweets (hard candy), apples, bread and butter, bread and jam, rose-hip syrup.**

The proper order would be (sugar contents in brackets): cheddar cheese (0.0), 'diet' drink (0.0), bread and butter (about 1.4), glass of milk (4.7), an apple (10.5), cola drink (10.1), bread and jam (about 19), rose-hip syrup (61.8), boiled sweets (86.9).

I have placed the 'diet' drink above cheese because it contains acid. The bread-and-jam figure is based on a quarter of the weight being jam, but this is variable depending on the thickness of the slice, and the amount of jam. The cola drink is placed above apple because it contains sucrose and all the sugar is free to circulate in the mouth, whereas much of the apple sugar is inside the pieces swallowed. Rose-hip syrup is quoted undiluted – if diluted (12.2), it would come before bread and jam. Boiled sweets are worst because of highest sugar content, and also because when sucked, **they stay in the mouth longest.**

As to which of these foods are safe, I would say that cheese to milk are completely safe, the apple has an intermediate position (not a good idea last thing at night, for example – it contains acid as well as sugar), and from cola up they are all bad for the teeth, if there is any plaque present, which there nearly always is.

CHAPTER 9 – FLUORIDE AND FISSURE SEALANTS

1. **Can fluoride ever be dangerous?**

   Yes it can, like almost anything else which passes through the mouth, if it is taken in too high a quantity. Studies have shown that even in areas where 8 p.p.m. of fluoride exists (remember that 1 p.p.m. is the 'ideal' in temperate climates) naturally in the water supply, no increase in illness of any kind can be detected compared with that in low fluoride areas. But such findings are based on people drinking 'normal' amounts of liquid in temperate climates, say 1 litre per day for an adult. Field workers in very hot climates can easily drink 8 litres of water a day and lose most of it in perspiration. Under those extreme conditions a dangerous accumulation might eventually occur from water fluoride levels as low as 2 p.p.m. (i.e. 2 mg fluoride per litre). The most common effect is 'fluorosis' of the bones in which the bones become more heavily mineralized and more brittle so that spontaneous fractures can occur. Also some of the ligaments joining the vertebrae may calcify giving rise to stiffness of the spine. However, these effects result only from prolonged intake of say 16 mg fluoride per day (8 litres of water), and with fluid loss through perspiration rather than through the kidneys, and not from the 1 mg or so contained in a typical day's fluid intake in temperate or cold climates.

2. **Can your dentist fluoridate your teeth for you?**

   Yes he can using solutions gels or varnishes containing high concentrations of fluoride. It used to be thought that this was a most important aid to decay prevention. Nowadays the opinion is growing that the daily intake of low concentrations of fluoride at home – in the form of toothpaste or fluoride rinses – is even more effective than these strong solutions applied every few months by the dentist. So the use of high-concentrations of fluoride tends to be reserved for people who have unusually high decay rates or who have difficulty in using fluoride toothpaste effectively (disabled or handi-capped people).

3. **What advantage is there in letting fluoride tablets dissolve in the mouth?**

   The advantage is that the solution of fluoride in the mouth bathes the visible tooth surfaces making them stronger before the remaining fluoride is swallowed and built into the developing teeth.

4. **If you are giving fluoride supplements to your child, does it matter if he eats toothpaste?**

   It might, if he eats a lot of toothpaste. The fluoride in this, if added to what you are providing with tablets or drops, may take the level above the optimum daily level for your child's weight. There would then be a small risk of the teeth having tiny white specks on the enamel. To avoid this, just make sure that your children use toothpaste not more than about the size of a pea on their brushes, and spit it out. If you think your child has eaten fluoride toothpaste, omit the fluoride supplement that day and make the toothpaste less accessible.

C. A list of sugar contents of foods and drinks

Two principal sources of information have been used: the compendious British reference book, McCance and Widdowson's *The composition of foods* by A.A. Paul and D.A.T. Southgate (4th edition, Her Majesty's Stationery Office, £18) and an American paperback *Brand name guide to sugar* by Ira L. Shannon (1977, Nelson Hall $1.95). One difference between these two books is that Professor Shannon, an American dentist, has given the sucrose contents only, on the basis that he thinks sucrose is more harmful than other sugars, whereas the British book lists total sugar content; that is, sucrose and other sugars combined. Another difference is that many brands of prepared food listed in the American book are not sold in Britain, and vice versa. Even where the same brand is sold both sides of the Atlantic, one cannot assume identical sucrose concentration. In America the availability of glucose (corn) syrup, manufactured from the abundant maize crop, makes it cheaper than sucrose as a food additive. In Britain the reverse is true, so that, for the moment, sucrose contents are likely to be higher.

A third source of information was an article in the *Journal of Human Nutrition* (1978, pp. 335–47) by D.A.T. Southgate and others, which gives contents of all the different sugars in some foods and drinks.

Finally, I have been given a selected list compiled for the St Thomas Health District in London. This list, prepared by Issy Cole-Hamilton, differs from the others, in that the sugar content is expressed not in percentages but in the form of 5 gram teaspoons of sugar contained in stated portions of the food or drink. Since publication of the first edition of this book which gave only sugar percentages, several

150

dietitians have assured me that many people can visualize teaspoons of sugar more easily than percentages. It has proved impractical to convert the sugar contents of all the approximately 400 foods and drinks in my list to spoonsful, so, as a compromise, I have made a selection of items and expressed them in teaspoons, with the hope that the reader can use that as a guide to visualizing the percentages which appear in the main list.

A SELECTION OF FOODS AND DRINKS WITH THEIR SUGAR CONTENTS EXPRESSED IN PERCENTAGES OF THEIR WEIGHT AND ALSO IN TEASPOONS

	Percentage of sugar	Portion size and weight in grams (1 oz = 28g)	5g teaspoons of sugar in one portion (approx)
Commercial baby food desserts			
Heinz 'Pure Fruit' (no added sugar), 4 flavours	11.7–13.7	1 can, 128g	3
Heinz Junior Babyfood Dessert: egg custard with tapioca	7.4	1 can, 128g	2
Breakfast cereals			
Sugar Puffs	56.5	6 tbs, 20g	2
Shredded Wheat	0.4	1 biscuit, 15g	Trace
Cereals			
Spaghetti, canned in tomato sauce	3.4	1 can, 440g	3
Boiled rice	Trace	any size	Trace
Bread			
Baby rusks	15–31.2	1 rusk, 17g	½–1
Wholemeal	2.1	1 slice, 30g	Trace
Milk and milk products			
Fruit yoghurt	17.9	1 sm. carton 150g	5
Cottage cheese	1.4	1 sm. carton 113g	⅓

151

Good mouthkeeping

	Percentage sugar	Portion size	Teaspoons of sugar
Confectionery			
Peppermints	97.2	1 bag, 113g	22
Mars bar	65.8	1 bar, 68g	9
Milk chocolate	56.5	1 sm. bar, 60g	7
Chewing gum	74.6	1 pack, 25g	4
Fresh fruit			
Apple, eating	10.5	1 medium, 100g	2
Watermelon	5.3	1 slice, 200g	2
Canned fruit			
Apricots	27.7	1 sm. can, 250g	14
Grapefruit	15.5	1 sm. can, 250g	8
Dried fruit			
Sultanas	64.7	1 handful, 60g	8
Figs	52.9	1 handful, 60g	6
Soft drinks			
Lucozade	19.3	1 sm. glass, 200g	8
Ribena (diluted 1:4)	15.2	1 sm. glass, 200g	6
Cola drink	10.1	1 can, 330g	6½
Diet cola drink	0	any amount	0
Alcoholic drinks			
Liqueur	29.8	1 measure, 20g	1
Lager beer	1.5	1 can, 330g	1
Preserves			
Honey	76.4	2 tsp, 15g	2
Peanut butter	6.7	3 tsp, 30g	½
Puddings (sweets, desserts)			
Ice-cream, non-dairy	19.7	1 sm. block, 330g	12
Cheesecake	13.9	1 piece, 150g	4
Chocolate sauce	72.0	3 tsp, 15g	2

List of sugar contents

Buns and pastries			
Jam tart	37.5	1 tart, 30g	2
Doughnut	23.8	1 piece, 40g	2
Sauces and pickles			
Tomato ketchup	22.9	4 tsp. 20g	1
Salad cream	13.4	4 tsp. 20g	$\frac{1}{2}$

COMMERCIAL BABY FOODS

Most manufacturers are extremely coy about stating the sugar contents of their products. Heinz is an honourable exception, giving, on request, clear unequivocal figures for each of its baby foods. The other manufacturers provide lists of what their products contain, what they do not contain, but rarely the quantities of anything. When they do give quantities, the sugar content is apt to be hidden within a figure for total carbohydrate, often expressed in kilojoules of energy, which defeats the keenest sugar hound.

A nutritional comparison of infant formulae available in the UK (produced by Farley Health Products – a Glaxo Group Company – January 1982) shows that, when reconstituted, all had sugar contents very close to that of mature human milk (7.2 per cent). The products analysed were SMA and SMA Goldcap (Wyeth), Osterfeed, Ostermilk Complete Formula and Ostermilk Two (Farley), Premium and Plus (Cow & Gate) and Milumil (Milupa).

In 1978 Professor Shannon reported his analysis of 69 American baby foods from three manufacturers (Heinz, Gerber, and Beech-Nut). The average sugar content in baby desserts was 9.2 with a range from 4.3 to 16.3 per cent. Today's figures would probably be lower because American parents have become very sugar-conscious.

The up-to-date total sugar content in the Heinz range as sold in the UK is as follows:

Dried weaning food desserts 2.6–4.7% (when made up)
Strained baby food desserts 6.5–9.9%
Baby desserts in jars 6.1–9.9%
Junior baby food desserts 5.1–10.0%
'Pure fruit' dessert (no added sugar) 11.7–13.1%

153

MAIN LIST

The sugar contents are given as a **percentage of the weight**. Total sugars are given first, with sucrose content in brackets after, where available. Since they are placed in descending order of sugar content, try to pick your foods from the end of each section.

It is not possible to give you a safety limit for the teeth. Variables, such as how long the food or drink stays in the mouth, the size of the pieces swallowed, and how much the saliva flow is stimulated, make such a generalization unreliable. Just cut down on the sugar levels, and especially the number of times a day you or your children have sugar-containing food.

Food and drinks with sugar expressed as percentage of weight. Sucrose content is in brackets.

Breakfast cereals

Sugar Puffs	56.5 (45.6)	Rice Krispies	9.0 (7.7)
Muesli	26.2 (10.6)	Cornflakes	7.4 (2.5)
Sugar frosted cornflakes	(15.6 – 32.2)	Weetabix	6.1
All Bran	15.4 (12.1)	Ready Brek	2.2 (1.4)
Special K	9.6 (5.8)	Puffed Wheat	1.5 (0.6)
Grapenuts	9.5 (0.0)	Shredded Wheat	0.4 (0.3)

Comment. Sugar is often added to these at home, which increases the percentage.

Cereals

Baby rusks	15.0–31.2	Flour, plain white	1.7
		self-raising	1.4
Bemax	16.0	Macaroni	Trace
Soya flour	11.2–13.4	Oatmeal	Trace
Bran	3.8	Porridge	Trace
Spaghetti canned in tomato sauce	3.4	Rice and rice flour	Trace
Spaghetti	2.7	Sago flour	Trace
Flour 100%	2.3	Semolina	Trace
85%	1.9	Tapioca	Trace

List of sugar contents

Bread

Malt	18.6	Brown	1.8
Currant	13.0	White	1.8
Soda	3.0	Chapatis	1.8
Hovis	2.4	Starch Reduced	1.6
Wholemeal	2.1		

Beverages

Drinking chocolate	73.8 (73.8)		
Ovaltine	73.0	Cocoa powder	Trace
Coffee & chicory essence	53.8 (47.5)	Coffee ground, infused	Trace
Bournvita	52.0	Tea	Trace
Horlicks	49.4	Instant coffee	0.0

Comment. The addition of two teaspoons of granulated sugar to a cup of coffee or tea gives a sucrose content of 10 per cent. If the cocoa is made with milk, two spoons of sugar will give a final sugar concentration of 14 per cent.

Confectionery

Peppermints	97.2	Pastilles	61.9
Boiled sweets (hard candy)	86.9	Plain chocolate	59.5 (58.7)
		Milk chocolate	56.5 (52.0)
Chewing gum	74.6 (60)	Bounty bar	53.7
Toffees	70.1	Fruit gums	42.6
Liquorice Allsorts	67.2	Orbit chewing gum	0
Fancy filled chocolates	65.8	Trident chewing gum	0
Mars bar	65.8		

Comment
1. The sugar-free chewing gums are absolutely safe for teeth. All other products listed are damaging. The range of sugar-free confectionery is much greater in North America.
2. The time for which sugar is present in the mouth will be greater for sweets when they are sucked, than when they are chewed and swallowed.

Biscuits

Wafers (filled)	44.7 (42.9)	Shortbread	17.2
Chocolate-coated	43.4 (38.2)	Digestive	16.4
Ginger nuts	35.8 (32.8)	Wheat starch	
Sandwich (e.g.		reduced	
custard creams)	30.2 (27.8)	(Energen)	7.4 (0)
Chocolate		Matzo	4.2 (0)
digestive	28.5 (26.0)	Rye crispbread	
Semisweet		(Ryvita)	3.2 (1.3)
(Osborne,		Water biscuits	2.3
Rich Tea)	22.3 (19.1)	Cream Crackers	Trace

Cakes

Fruit-cake,		Fruit cake	
iced with		(e.g. Dundee)	46.7 (20.5)
marzipan	54.2	Madeira	36.5 (35.5)
Fancy iced	54.0 (47.8)	Gingerbread	31.8
Jam-filled		Rock cakes	31.3
sponge	47.7 (35.7)	Sponge cake	30.9

Buns and pastries

Jam tarts	37.5	Scotch pancakes	8.1
Mince pies	30.0	Scones	6.1
Chocolate eclairs	26.3	Pastry	
Doughnuts	23.8	(choux, flaky,	
Currant buns	14.0	shortcrust)	0.4–1.2

Puddings

Meringues	95.6	Suet pudding	14.0
Jelly, packet cubes	62.6	Cheesecake	13.9
Christmas pudding	39.1	Bread and butter	
Treacle tart	33.6	pudding	12.0
Fruit pie	30.9 (21.5)	Custard made	
Queen of puddings	28.9	with powder	11.5
Lemon meringue pie	24.8	Egg custard	11.0
Apple crumble	23.8	Milk pudding —	
Ice-cream: dairy	22.6 (14.5)	rice, sago, tapioca	10.9
non-dairy	19.7 (14.6)	Canned rice	8.9 (5.1)
Sponge pudding	18.9	Custard tart	6.0
Jelly made with		Yorkshire	3.8
water	14.2	Dumpling	0.5

List of sugar contents

Sugars

Demerara	100.00	Black treacle	67.2
White	100.00	Liquid glucose	
Golden Syrup	79.0	BP	40.2

Preserves

Honey	76.4	Glacé cherries	55.8
Marmalade	69.5	Marzipan	49.2
Jam	69.3	Lemon curd	40.4 (12.0)
Mincemeat	62.1	Peanut butter	6.7 (6.7)

Sauces and pickles

Apple chutney	50.1	Brown sauce	23.1
Tomato chutney	39.5	Tomato ketchup	22.9
Sweet pickle		Salad cream	13.4
(Branston &		Tomato puree	11.4
Pan Yan)	32.6 (3.4)	Piccalilli	2.6 (0.1)

Soft drinks, fruit and vegetable juices

Rose-hip syrup, undiluted	61.8 (44.2)	15.5 ⎫
Ribena, undiluted	60.9	15.2 ⎪ diluted
Orange drink, undiluted	28.5	7.1 ⎬ 1 in 4
Lime juice cordial undiluted	24.8	6.2 ⎭
Lucozade	19.3	
Pineapple juice, canned	13.4	
Orange juice, canned sweetened	12.8	
Cola drink	10.1 (0.5)	
Grapefruit juice, canned sweetened	9.7 (0.3)	
Orange juice, canned unsweetened	8.5 (2.3)	
Grapefruit juice, canned unsweetened	7.9 (0.3)	
*Fanta orange drink	(4.4)	
*7-Up	(4.1)	
Tomato juice, canned	3.2 (0.1)	
V-8 vegetable juice	(0.2)	

*These soft drinks are not listed in McCance & Widdowson and therefore only show as sucrose content. They probably have a total sugar-content similar to that of Cola drinks.

Alcoholic drinks

Liqueurs	29.8	Medium white wine	3.4
Advocaat	28.4 (26.7)	Dry cider	2.6
Port	12.0	Rosé wine	2.5 (0)
Sweet vermouth	15.9 (3.7)	Bitter beer	2.5
Vintage cider	7.3	Lager beer	1.5
Sweet sherry	6.9	Sparkling white wine	1.4
Barley wine	6.1	Dry sherry	1.4
Sweet white wine	5.9	Dry white wine	0.6 (0)
Dry vermouth	5.5 (1.6)	Red wine	0.3
Medium sherry	3.6 (0)	Spirits	Trace

Diet drinks (low calorie) — information from cans

Diet Pepsi	0.0	Schweppes	
Diet 7-Up	0.0	Slimline drinks	0.0
Energen 'One Cal'		Weight Watchers	
drinks	0.0	Low calorie	
Fresca	0.0	drinks	0.0

Meat	—	**NO SUGARS**	**Eggs**	—	**NO SUGARS**
Fish	—	**NO SUGARS**	**Fats**	—	**NO SUGARS**

Fruits — dried or canned

Sultanas, dried	64.7	Peaches, canned	22.9
Raisins, dried	64.4	Raspberries, canned	22.5
Dates, dried	63.9	Strawberries,	
Currants, dried	63.1	canned	21.1 (7.0)
Peaches, dried	53.0	Mangos, canned	20.2 (4.4)
Figs, dried	52.9	Pineapple, canned	20.2
Apricots, dried	43.4	Pears, canned	20.0
Prunes, dried	40.3	Lychees, canned	17.7 (0.6)
Apricots, canned	27.7	Paw paw, canned	17.0 (2.0)
Loganberries,		Guavas, canned	15.7 (3.7)
canned	26.2	Grapefruit, canned	15.5 (1.9)
Fruit salad, canned	25.0	Mandarines,	
Fruit pie filling		canned	14.2 (3.4)
canned	23.0	Oranges, canned	12.8

Comment

1. The high sugar-content of dried fruit is the direct result of water loss.
2. Canned fruit has an average of 12 per cent more sugar than the equivalent fresh fruit.

List of sugar contents

Fruit stewed with sucrose 11.4–19.7

Apples, blackberries, cherries, currants (black, white, and red), damsons, gooseberries, greengages, loganberries pears, plums, raspberries, rhubarb.

Comment

Stewed fruit has an average of 8.8 per cent more sugar than the equivalent fresh fruit.

Fresh fruit

Bananas	16.2 (6.6)	Oranges	8.5 (3.7)
Lychees	16.0	Apricots	8.3 (5.8)
White grapes	15.5 (0.5)	Mulberries	8.1
Mangos	15.3	Tangerines	8.0
Black grapes	14.4 (0.5)	Blackberries	6.4 (0.5)
Bilberries	14.3	Quinces	6.3
Nectarines	12.4	Raspberries	6.2 (2.0)
Cherries	11.9 (0.2)	Passion fruit	6.2
Greengages	11.8	Strawberries	5.9 (1.1)
Pineapple	11.6 (7.9)	White currants	5.6 (1.1)
Pomegranates	11.6	Grapefruit	5.3 (2.1)
Plums, eating	11.2 (4.9)	Melon,	
Medlars	10.6	canteloupe	5.3 (3.3)
Apples, eating	10.5 (3.0)	Watermelon	5.3 (2.4)
Black currants	10.4 (1.0)	Melon,	
Damsons	9.6 (1.0)	honeydew	5.0 (1.4)
Pears	9.5 (1.3)	Red currants	4.4 (0.5)
Figs	9.5	Cranberries	3.5
Gooseberries, ripe	9.2 (1.1)	Loganberries	3.4 (0.2)
Peaches	8.7 (6.6)	Lemon (juice)	1.6 (0.2)

Vegetables

Of 100 vegetables listed in McCance & Widdowson

Average sugar content = 2.7 per cent (S.D. = 2.56)

and the sugar range was 0 per cent (mushrooms) to 11.5 (fried ripe plantain).

Milk and milk products

Condensed, skimmed, sweetened	60.0	Yoghurt, fruit	17.9 (10.2)
		Yoghurt, hazelnut	16.5 (10.2)
Condensed, whole sweetened	55.5 (45.3)	Yoghurt, flavoured	14.0 (7.9)

all the above contain added sucrose

Evaporated, whole unsweetened	11.3	Goats' milk	4.6
Human milk,	7.2	Cream, single	3.2
mature transitional	6.9	sterilized canned	2.7
Natural yoghurt	6.2	whipping	2.5
Cows milk		double	2.0
fresh skimmed	5.0	Cheese, cottage	1.4
fresh whole	4.7	cheese spread	0.9
sterilized	4.7	other types	Trace
long-life UHT treated	4.7	Butter	Trace

MEDICINES FOR BABIES AND YOUNG CHILDREN

Doctors are often reluctant to prescribe tablets for children when the required dose is less than the lowest dose tablet available. The difficulties of dividing a tablet and, for very young children, the difficulty in swallowing tablets has provided a market for liquid preparations of drugs. Unfortunately manufacturers have been inclined to use concentrated sugar syrups as vehicles for these preparations because sugar is cheap, it masks the flavour of the active ingredients and, in high concentration, it protects the medicine against spoilage.

A helpful document produced by the National Pharmaceutical Association in the UK lists 222 liquid oral preparations (suspensions, elixirs, mixtures, syrups, liquids, etc.) of which only 50 are sugar-free. The remainder have sugar concentrations ranging between 30 and 80 per cent. The use of these latter may not have a great impact on dental health in short-term drug treatments, say a week or two, but some children have chronic illnesses which require long-term treatment with drugs. Where sugar/syrup-based preparations have to be used in preference to tablets or capsules, the dental damage can be very serious. One study of children taking such medicines daily for six months

(Roberts, I.F., Roberts, G.J., *British Medical Journal* 1979, Vol 2, p.14) showed that they had four times as much tooth decay as children who were taking tablets or no medicines.

Not all medical practitioners are aware of this risk, and so, to help parents who receive prescriptions for their children, I have prepared a list of drugs by type, showing the numbers of liquid oral preparations with and without sugar, and naming those which are sugar-free. The principal sources are the National Pharmaceutical Association list (1984) mentioned above, and the British National Formulary No 7 (1984).

The brand names of identical formulations made by one manufacturer may vary in different countries, so this list is of most relevance in the UK. But this does not prevent interested parents in other countries asking the doctor for sugar-free versions of liquid medicines. If there is no sugar-free alternative, and tablets or capsules cannot be used, toothbrushing with a fluoride toothpaste immediately after taking the syrup will reduce the risk to teeth. This applies equally to those on long-term medication and to those taking short courses of antibiotics or cough syrups.

The brand name of the medicine is given first, with the name and concentration of the active ingredients in brackets following. A standard medicine spoon contains 5 ml. An asterisk denotes that the preparation is obtainable without prescription in the UK.

ANTIBIOTICS AND OTHER DRUGS USED AGAINST INFECTIONS

PENICILLINS

Penicillinase-sensitive penicillins

23 with sugar, none without

Penicillinase-resistant penicillins

2 with sugar, none without

Broad-spectrum penicillins

16 with sugar, 4 without

Augmentin, junior suspension (amoxycillin 125 mg/5 ml)
Augmentin, paediatric suspension (amoxycillin 125 mg/5 ml)
Ampiclox Neonatal (ampicillin 60 mg, cloxacillin 30 mg/0.6 ml must be given with a pipette)
Pondocillin, suspension (pivampicillin 162 mg/5 ml)

CEPHALOSPORINS AND CEPHAMYCINS

13 with sugar, none without

TETRACYCLINES

6 with sugar, 2 without

Ledermycin syrup (demeclocycline 75 mg/5 ml)
Vibramycin syrup (doxycycline 50 mg/5 ml)

N.B. Tetracyclines can make developing teeth permanently yellow-grey, and are therefore not recommended for children before the age of 12 years. By that age tablets can be prescribed instead of the sugary syrups in most cases.

List of sugar-free liquid oral medicines

AMINOGLYCOSIDES

none with sugar, 1 without

Neomycin elixir BPC (100 mg/5 ml)

ERYTHROMYCIN

9 with sugar, none without

CLINDAMYCIN AND LINCOMYCIN

2 with sugar, none without

OTHER ANTIBIOTICS

4 with sugar, none without

SULPHONAMIDES AND TRIMETHOPRIM

12 with sugar, 4 without

Trimethoprim mixture BP (50 mg/5 ml)
Ipral paediatric suspension (trimethoprim 50 mg/5 ml)
Monotrim suspension   ('   '   '   )
Trimopan suspension   ('   '   '   )

ANTI-TUBERCULOUS DRUGS

3 with sugar, 1 without

Isoniazid Elixir BPC (50 mg/5 ml)

METRONIDAZOLE

1 with sugar, none without

URINARY ANTIMICROBIAL DRUGS

5 with sugar, 2 without

Furadantin suspension (nitrofurantoin 25 mg/5 ml)
Negram suspension (nalixidic acid 300 mg/5 ml)

ANTIFUNGAL DRUGS

4 with sugar, 2 without

Fungilin suspension (amphotericin 100 mg/ml)
Pimafucin, oral suspension (natamycin 10 mg/ml)

ANTIMALARIALS

2 with sugar, none without

DRUGS FOR THREADWORMS

5 with sugar, none without

DRUGS FOR ROUNDWORMS

1 with sugar, none without

DRUGS USED FOR THE RESPIRATORY SYSTEM

BRONCHODILATORS

Selective beta$_2$-adrenoceptor stimulants

2 with sugar, 3 without

Bricanyl syrup (terbutaline 1.5 mg/5 ml)
Bronchodil elixir (reproterol hydrochloride 10 mg/5 ml)
Ventolin syrup (salbutamol 2 mg/5 ml)

List of sugar-free liquid oral medicines

Non-selective adrenoceptor stimulants

none with sugar, 1 without

Alupent syrup (orciprenaline 10 mg/5 ml)

Anticholinergic bronchodilators

none with sugar, 1 without

Eumydrin drops (atropine methonitrate 0.6%)

Xanthine bronchodilators

5 with sugar, none without

Oral mucolytics

4 with sugar, 1 without

Bisolvon elixir (bromhexine hydrochloride 4 mg/5 ml)
BISOLVON)

Compound bronchodilator preparations

2 with sugar, 2 without

Bricanyl Expectorant (guaiphenesin 66.5 mg and terbutaline 1.5 mg/5 ml)
Tedral elixir (ephedrine 6 mg and theophylline 30 mg/5 ml)

CONTROL OF ASTHMA

1 with sugar, none without

ANTIHISTAMINES

10 with sugar, 1 without

Tavegil elixir (clemastine 500 micrograms/5 ml)

COUGH SUPPRESSANTS

13 with sugar, 2 without

*Codeine Linctus Diabetic, BPC (codeine 15 mg/5 ml)
*Dia-tuss syrup (pholcodeine 10 mg/5 ml)

EXPECTORANTS, DEMULCENTS, AND COMPOUND PREPARATIONS ('COUGH MEDICINES')

62 with sugar, 12 without

Alupent Expectorant
*Ammonia and ipecacuana mixture BP
*Ammonium chloride mixture BP
*Ammonium chloride and morphine mixture BP
*Boots Bronchial Cough Mixture
Extil Compound linctus
*Ipecacuana and morphine mixture BP
*Pavacol-D mixture
*Pholcomed Diabetic linctus
*Pholcomed Forte Diabetic linctus
*Pholtex mixture
Tedral Expectorant
(N.B. The cough medicines above and decongestants below are mixtures of many things, too complex to annotate)

SYSTEMIC NASAL DECONGESTANTS

9 with sugar, 4 without

*Dimotapp elixir
*Dimotapp paediatric elixir
*Eskornade syrup
*Triogesic elixir

GASTRO-INTESTINAL DRUGS

ANTACIDS (These contain various mixtures)

23 with sugar, 16 without

*Actal suspension
*Aluminium Hydroxide Mixture BP

List of sugar-free liquid oral medicines

* Altacite suspension
* Altacite Plus suspension
* Asilone for Infants
* Dijex liquid
* Diovol suspension
* Diovol Fruit suspension
* Gelusil suspension
* Infant Gaviscon
* Maalox suspension
* Maalox Plus suspension
* Magnesium Carbonate Mixture BPC
* Magnesium Carbonate Mixture, Aromatic, BP
* Magnesium Hydroxide Mixture, BP
* Magnesium Trisilicate Mixture, BP

ANTISPASMODICS

17 with sugar, 7 without

* Aluminium Hydroxide and Belladonna Mixture, BPC (belladonna alkaloids 300 micrograms/10 ml)
Eumydrin drops (atropine methonitrate 200 micrograms/drop)
* Kolanticon Gel (dicyclomine hydrochloride 2.5 mg/5 ml plus antacids)
* Kolantyl Gel (dicyclomine hydrochloride 2.5 mg/5 ml plus antacids)
Maxolon syrup (metoclopramide 5 mg/5 ml)
Maxolon Paediatric liquid (metoclopramide 1 mg/ml)
* Magnesium Trisilicate and Belladonna Mixture, BPC (belladonna alkaloids 150 micrograms/10 ml)

ULCER-HEALING DRUGS

2 with sugar, none without

ANTI-DIARRHOEAL DRUGS

10 with sugar, 6 without

* Imodium syrup (loperamide 1 mg/5 ml)
* Kaodene mixture (codeine phosphate 10 mg, light kaolin 3 g/10 ml)
* Kaolin Mixture BP
* Kaolin and Morphine Mixture BP
* Kaopectate mixture (kaolin 1.03 g/5 ml)
Lomotil liquid (diphenoxylate 2.5 mg, atropine 25 micrograms/5 ml)

LAXATIVES (BULK-FORMING)

13 with sugar, 1 without

*Normacol Standard Sugar-free Formula
(N.B. With regard to other laxative groups – stimulant, softening and osmotic laxatives – I was unable to get information on the sugar contents)

DRUGS ACTING ON THE CENTRAL NERVOUS SYSTEM

HYPNOTICS AND SEDATIVES

6 with sugar, 1 without

Heminevrin syrup (chlormethiazole 250 mg/5 ml)

ANXIOLYTICS

1 with sugar, 2 without

Diazepam Elixir (2 mg/5 ml)
Valium Syrup (diazepam 2 mg/5 ml)

NEUROLEPTICS

12 with sugar, 3 without

Haldol oral liquid (haloperidol 2 mg/ml)
Serenace oral liquid (haloperidol 2 mg/ml)
Stelazine syrup (trifluoperazine 1 mg/5 ml)

ANTIDEPRESSANT DRUGS (TRYCYCLIC)

2 with sugar, 3 without

Aventyl liquid (nortriptyline 10 mg/5 ml)
Molipaxin liquid (trazodone hydrochloride 50 mg/5 ml
Triptizol mixture (amitriptyline 10 mg/5 ml)

List of sugar-free liquid oral medicines

PREVENTION OF NAUSEA (E.G. WITH CYTOTOXIC DRUGS)

none with sugar, 1 without

Motilium suspension (domperidone 5 mg/5 ml)

NON-NARCOTIC ANALGESICS ('PAIN KILLERS')

8 with sugar, 6 without

Brufen syrup (ibuprofen 100 mg/5 ml)
*Benoral suspension (benorylate 2 g/5 ml)
Indocid suspension (indomethacin 25 mg/5 ml)
*Paracetamol Elixir, Paediatric, BP (120 mg/5 ml)
*Sodium Salicylate Mixture, BP (250 mg/5 ml)
*Sodium Salicylate Mixture, Strong BP (500 mg/5 ml)

NARCOTIC ANALGESICS FOR MILD TO MODERATE PAIN

2 with sugar, none without

COMPOUND ANALGESIC PREPARATIONS

2 with sugar, none without

ANTIEPILEPTICS

6 with sugar, 3 without

Epilim syrup (sodium valproate 200 mg/5 ml)
Tegretol Syrup (carbamazepine 100 mg/5 ml)
Phenobarbitone Elixir, BP (30 mg/10 ml)

CARDIOVASCULAR DRUGS

CARDIAC GLYCOSIDES

2 with sugar, none without

DIURETICS

none with sugar, 2 without

Burinex liquid (bumetanide 1 mg/5 ml)
Lasix Paediatric liquid (frusemide 1 mg/ml)

ANTIHYPERTENSIVE DRUGS

1 with sugar, none without

PERIPHERAL VASODILATORS

none with sugar, 1 without

*Hexopal suspension (inositol nicotinate 1 g/5 ml)

DRUGS AFFECTING NUTRITION AND BLOOD

IRON THERAPY

12 with sugar, 2 without

*Niferex elixir (100 mg ferrous iron/5 ml)
*Sytron Elixir (27.5 mg iron equivalent/5 ml)

MEGALOBLASTIC ANAEMIA

none with sugar, 1 without

Lexpec syrup (folic acid 2.5 mg/5 ml)

VITAMINS

In the British National Formulary (1983) 19 vitamins supplement liquids are described, most of which contain sugar. The exceptions may be One-alpha Drops, and calciferol solution (in oil) both of which increase vitamin D levels in the blood. Ketovite supplement for synthetic diets may also be sugar-free.

The routine use of vitamin supplements as a general 'pick-me-up' without medical supervision is of doubtful value and, in the case of vitamins A and D, may be dangerous.

D. Glossary

DENTAL TERMS

(in the definitions, words in **bold** type are defined elsewhere in the glossary)

amalgam (a-**mal**-gum): a powdered alloy of silver, tin, zinc, and copper, mixed with mercury to form a mouldable material which becomes strong enough to bite on after a few hours. Very good filling material if properly used. Providing you don't get **secondary caries**, an amalgam filling should last for 20 years or more. Very big ones tend to break, because the material doesn't have a high tensile strength.

bridge: a fixed replacement of a missing tooth or teeth. The artificial tooth (called the 'pontic') is joined to one or more crowns which are cemented to nearby teeth. Because of the time taken to grind these teeth accurately, to make the bridge in the dental laboratory, and the cost of the materials, these replacements are expensive. In Britain they **can** be made on the National Health Service, but the dentist would have to get special permission for this, which is not always granted; and if it is, he may not think the NHS fee is high enough. They should only be used where a patient has very good **oral hygiene** and a suitable low sugar diet. Otherwise, continuing gum disease or tooth decay make them expensive failures.

calculus (**cal**-cue-lus): the technical name for the tartar or scale which forms on teeth, especially opposite the openings of the main saliva glands (inside lower front teeth, outside upper back teeth). Formed from mineralized plaque built up in layers, with calcium salts deposited in it from saliva. It does not harm the teeth, but it indirectly harms the gums by providing a rough surface to which plaque sticks easily and from which it is difficult to remove.

caries (**care**-is): technical term for dental decay.

cement: 1. a very thin layer of bone-like material present on the outside of the root. This may decay in **root caries**.
2. a material used by dentists to fix crowns and other things onto teeth, and occasionally used as a temporary filling material.

composite: a mixture of a plastic material which sets, and finely-powdered

172

glass or quartz added to make it harder and stronger and more wear-resistant. Its optical and thermal expansion properties are similar to those of teeth, so it looks quite good and doesn't leak much around the edges. Used mostly as a front tooth filling material, because **amalgam** is a better material where appearance is not so important. Amalgam can be made very smooth and easy to clean. Composite is always slightly rough and therefore not a good idea if placed next to the gum.

crown: 1. the visible part of the tooth.

2. an artificial tooth-shaped cap put over the natural crown of a tooth after some of it has been ground away to make space. The materials used for this are porcelain, porcelain bonded to gold, and gold (for back teeth). Plastic is used for **temporary crowns and bridges** (see **jacket crown** and **post crown**).

dental floss: a multifilament thread used for removing plaque or food from teeth and from under bridges. Can be bought at most chemists and is available waxed or unwaxed, according to individual preference. Dental tape is a wider version of the same. Floss is also used to detect **overhangs**.

dentifrice (**den**-ti-friss): old-fashioned technical term for toothpastes and powders.

dentine (**den**-teen) the softer, but still quite strong, material from which the major part of the crown and root of the natural tooth are made.

denture: a removable artificial replacement for missing natural teeth. Complete dentures (also called full dentures) are made for people who have no natural teeth remaining in one or both jaws. Partial dentures are made for jaws where some natural teeth remain. Dentures are rarely a completely satisfactory replacement for natural teeth.

enamel (en-**am**-el): the hard outer layer of the **natural crown**.

filling: lay term (dentists call it a 'restoration') for a material put into teeth after decay has been removed and a specially shaped hole has been made. **Amalgam** (silvery colour) is used most for back teeth, and **composite** (tooth colour) for front teeth. The main problem with fillings is that if a filling goes down the side of a tooth an **overhang** is often developed. Using a wedge to hold the bottom of the **matrix band** against the side of the tooth, when the filling material is being pressed in, will avoid this problem. All good dentists use wedges for this shape of filling.

floss: (see **dental floss**)

gingivitis (jin-jiv-**eye**-tis): technical name for gum inflammation.

gold: pure gold is too soft to use for **crowns** and **bridges**, so dental gold is an alloy in which platinum, palladium, iridium and some other metals are added to gold to give greater strength. Dental gold is about twice as expensive as pure gold. A rare kind of filling for small holes is carried out by a few dentists using pure gold foil. The reason why gold alloys are used at all for dentistry is that they are strong and will not tarnish or corrode in the mouth.

gumboil: the lay term for a dental abscess which has burst through the socket bone and made the overlying gum swell. Eventually it will discharge, usually into the mouth.

gum disease: also called periodontal disease. A slowly progressing inflammatory process caused by **plaque** in which bleeding and swelling of the edge of the gum are followed by gradual loss of the connection between root and socket, and finally by the loss of the bone itself and by looseness of the tooth. The major cause of tooth loss in Britain and elsewhere.

jacket crown: a **crown** which fits around a prepared tooth to restore the shape and appearance of the original. Made of porcelain or porcelain bonded to gold.

lining material: a kind of **cement** put underneath metal fillings as an insulator to stop very hot or very cold foods making the teeth hurt. (The white material the dentist puts in before the filling.)

matrix band (**may**-trix): the thin metal or plastric strip which holds a filling material to the shape of the tooth while it sets.

oral hygiene: the general term used for all the methods of plaque removal which you can use at home.

overhang: a ledge of filling material sticking out from the bottom of a filling when it does not follow the shape of the tooth. It can usually be best seen on an X-ray of the back teeth. It causes gum damage by making the plaque difficult or impossible to remove. If your floss frays a lot or breaks when being removed from between two particular teeth, you probably have an overhang. A good dentist can usually avoid creating overhangs by using wooden or plastic wedges between the teeth when putting in fillings. Sometimes, with very deep fillings, this is difficult to do without some minor gum surgery in the area.

periodontal disease: (see **gum disease**.)

plaque (rhymes with black or park): a mixture of bacteria, bacterial products and saliva components which forms on teeth and other hard surfaces in the mouth. It does not require the presence of food, though sugars make it form faster.

pocket: a crevice between the edge of the gum and the tooth. In health this is 2 mm deep or less. After gum disease it is often deeper, and may get so deep that the tooth becomes loose. Up to 4 mm deep it can probably be maintained by brushing and flossing without getting deeper. If more than that some gum surgery may be indicated, providing oral hygiene is good enough to make sure that the pockets will not form again.

post crown: a crown made to fit a tooth where the natural crown is not strong enough to hold a **jacket crown** because of previous decay. First a **root filling** is needed; than a post is made to fit down the root canal. To the top of this post the post crown is cemented. When people talk about 'screwing a crown into the gum' that is not what happens (except in a very few experimental centres). Actually the crown is cemented onto the post, which is cemented or screwed into the root.

pulp: proper technical term for the 'nerve' inside the tooth. Besides nerves it contains blood vessels, connective tissue and many kinds of cells.

pyorrhoea (pie-o-**rea**): old-fashioned name for **gum disease**.

radiograph (**ray**-dio-graf): the technical term for an X-ray picture. These are most useful and sometimes absolutely necessary in looking for early decay and other problems.

root: the part of the tooth below the gum level, mostly in bone.

root caries: a special type of decay which attacks the surface **cement** and underlying **dentine** of an exposed root. It is incompletely understood and tends to be found in older people. It should be preventable by a combination of minimal sugar intake, very careful daily cleaning and the use of fluoride rinses or toothpaste.

root filling: technique used in teeth with dead or dying **pulps**, often after deep decay. The pulp is numbed if still sensitive, then removed, and after the canal has been smoothed and cleaned, it is filled to block up the end and keep bacteria from getting into it. Often takes more than one appointment. Is usually preferable to extraction. (In North America the term 'root canal treatment', or its abbreviation 'a root canal', are used.)

rubber dam: a rubber sheet with specially punched holes placed over the teeth so that the crowns of certain teeth stick through. By doing this, the dentist can keep the teeth dry and improve visibility, thus improving the quality of his work. Occasionally it is not possible or advisable to use rubber dam. Not all dentists use this but those who do are probably rather good dentists.

saliva (sal-**eye**-ver): technical name for spittle. Saliva is very important in keeping the mouth clean, resisting infection and, as a lubricant, in making it easy to swallow, to taste food and to speak.

secondary caries: tooth decay which occurs around an existing filling or crown.

scaling: the removal of **calculus**, stains and other deposits from the tooth surface by dental instruments including ultrasonic scaling machines.

temporary crown or bridge: a **crown** or **bridge** made of plastic (or with back teeth, sometimes metal) used between the time when the teeth have been ground and the fitting of the permanent porcelain or gold crown(s).

temporary filling: a quickly-applied material for closing a hole until the dentist has time to do a permanent filling, or to give him time to see what will happen to the tooth. Most of these materials are based on zinc oxide powder mixed with oil of cloves, with other ingredients to make them set faster or become stronger. They do not hold up for a long time against chewing forces.

TYPES OF PERSONNEL IN THE DENTAL TEAM

Consultant
Strictly speaking, a senior person employed in a hospital to carry out particular specialities.
Three kinds of dental consultant exist in the British National Health Service: the oral surgeon, the restorative dentist, and the orthodontist. Some University (teaching) dentists have consultant status.

Dental health educator
In **Britain** a person who has gained a Royal Society of Health Diploma in Dental Health Education.
There are about 200 such people in Britain, to date, who organize dental health projects at schools and colleges, talk to PTA's, antenatal classes, play groups, etc.

Dental hygienist
A person qualified to instruct patients in plaque control and some other matters of dental health, to scale the crowns and accessible parts of the roots of teeth, to remove stains and other deposits, and to apply fluoride solutions and fissure sealants.
In **Britain** and many other parts of the world hygienists may only work under the direct supervision of a dentist who is in the office at the time. In the **United States** different States stipulate different degrees of supervision.

Dental laboratory technician
A person who has trained and become qualified to carry out the construction of various dentures, crowns, bridges, orthodontic appliances and other items used or worn in the mouth. This work is carried out away from the patient in a specially equipped laboratory.

Dental radiographer (US: Dental radiology technician)
A person specially trained to take X-rays. Dentists in general practice usually take their own X-rays.

Dental surgery assistant (US: Dental Assistant)
The correct name for the dental nurse (often shortened to DSA in Britain).

Dental therapist
In **Britain**, a person qualified to carry out the more simple fillings, in children and adolescents, teach them oral hygiene, apply fluoride and fissure sealants to the teeth, scale teeth, take X-rays, give certain anaesthetic injections and extract primary teeth under the supervision of a qualified dentist. Up

to the present, therapists work only in the public dental service (hospitals, community dental service, maternity and child welfare services).

In **Canada** the dental therapist can treat children and adults and, in addition to the role of the British therapist, can give mandibular nerve block injections, do pin-reinforced amalgam fillings and apply stainless steel crowns to primary teeth. In the North-West Territories and Saskatchewan, differences exist over a few other procedures.

In **Australia** there are seven different sets of State regulations about the activities of dental therapists, including different age ranges of patients. Roughly speaking they can do more than British therapists and less than Canadian therapists. All of them are taught to use rubber dam, give mandibular nerve blocks, scale teeth, do simple fillings, apply fluoride solutions, and extract primary teeth.

In **Hong Kong** the duties of a therapist are similar to those of the British therapist with the addition of the mandibular nerve block, and the extraction of permanent teeth.

Dental therapists are also trained in Fiji, Indonesia, Malaysia, Papua New Guinea, Singapore, Sri Lanka, Thailand, and the West Indies. The title of the New Zealand equivalent is School Dental Nurse (see separate entry).

Dentist

Someone who is qualified to practice dentistry. 'Dental surgeon' is an alternative name meaning exactly the same thing.

Endodontist

A dentist specializing in root canal treatment.

Expanded-function dental auxiliary

In the **USA**, someone originally qualified as a dental assistant who has subsequent training in the application of rubber dam, the application of fluoride solutions, the insertion of permanent and temporary filling materials into cavities cut by the dentist, and the provision of dental health education.

Expanded-function dental hygienist

Also in the **USA**, this individual would have qualified as a dental hygienist and then received further training. The result would be that in addition to her normal duties as a hygienist she would be entitled to do all that the expanded-function dental auxiliary does, and give local anaesthetic injections, light anaesthesia with nitrous oxide ('relative analgesia') and take impressions of the mouth for study casts.

Oral surgeon
A dentist, often with a medical qualification as well, who specializes in operations involving the teeth, soft tissues and bones of the jaws. The term 'maxillo-facial surgeon' implies involvement with areas a little beyond the mouth.

Orthodontist
A dentist who specializes in moving teeth with wires and bands to improve their health and appearance. Some regulation of the development of the face may also be involved.

Pedodontist
(Pea-do-dontist)
A dentist specializing in the treatment of children.

Periodontist
A dentist who specializes in promoting the health of gums.

Prosthetist
(Pros-thee-tist)
A dentist who specializes in replacing missing teeth, bone and gums with artificial ones.

Prosthodontist
North American term for prosthetist.

School Dental Nurse
The **New Zealand** equivalent of the **dental therapist**. This should really be phrased the other way round since the School Dental Nurses of New Zealand pre-date all the other therapists by more than 25 years. Their range of permitted activities is approximately that of the British therapists, with the differences that the School Dental Nurses treat children only up to 13 years, do not apply fissure sealants but can give mandibular nerve blocks.

E. What The Letters After Dentists' Names Mean

(Arranged in alphabetical order. The place of the University or other issuing body is sometimes shown abbreviated after the qualification. Degrees are awarded by Universities, Diplomas by a few Universities and some other bodies. The usual form of the qualification is here shown first, with variants in brackets.)

BDS (BChD, Bachelor of Dental Surgery (or Dental Science). A basic
BDentSc, University degree entitling a person to practise dentistry in
BDSc) the UK, the Republic of Ireland and parts of the British
Commonwealth.

BSc (BS in Bachelor of Science. A basic University degree in some science
N. America) subject. A few dentists have gained this extra degree before or
during their dental training.

DDS Doctor of Dental Surgery (or Dental Science).
(DChD, 1. DDS (DMD) is the basic qualification in North America.
DDSc) Some dentists working in other parts of the world but trained
in North America have this. All American dentists are called
'doctor'. British and Commonwealth dentists are called Mr,
Mrs, Miss, etc. unless they have a postgraduate doctoral
degree, e.g. a PhD or MD.
2. DDS (and variants) are awarded for postgraduate research in
the field of dentistry at some British and Commonwealth
Universities.

DOrth RCS Diploma in Orthodontics (or Dental Orthopaedics) of the
(DDOrth Royal College of Surgeons (or Royal College of Physicians and
RCPS, DDO Surgeons, or Royal Faculty of Physicians and Surgeons, both in
RFPS) Glasgow). Postgraduate diplomas awarded for specialist
training in orthodontics.

DDPH RCS Diploma in Dental Public Health (or Dental Health). A
(DDH, postgraduate diploma by one Royal College of Surgeons and a
DDPH, few Universities for studies in the dental health of
DPHD, communities.
DPD)

DRD RCS   Diploma in Restorative Dentistry of the Royal College of
Surgeons (of Edinburgh). A postgraduate diploma in some
major branches of general dentistry.

FDS RCS   Fellow in Dental Surgery of the Royal College of Surgeons (or
(FDS RCPS)   the Royal College of Physicians and Surgeons). A postgraduate
diploma indicating that a dentist has had further dental
training after qualification.

FFD RCS   Fellow of the Faculty of Dentistry of the Royal College of
Surgeons in Ireland. The Irish equivalent of FDS RCS.

FRACDS   Fellow of the Royal Australasian College of Dental Surgeons.
An Australian equivalent of FDS RCS.

FRCPath   Fellow of the Royal College of Pathologists. A postgraduate
diploma indicating specialist training and significant
experience in pathology. A few dentists have this.

FRCS   Fellow of the Royal College of Surgeons. A postgraduate
diploma like FDS RCS but in general rather than dental
surgery. Few dentists have this.

HDD RFPS   Higher Dental Diploma of the Royal Faculty of Physicians and
(HDD)   Surgeons (Glasgow) or Higher Diploma in Dentistry of the
University of Witwatersrand. A postgraduate diploma
approximately equivalent to FDS RCS.

LDS RCS   Licentiate in Dental Surgery of the Royal College of Surgeons
(LDS,   (or of a few Universities). A diploma entitling a person to
LDentSc)   practise dentistry. A basic qualification.

LRCP,   Licentiate of the Royal College of Physicians, Member of the
MRCS   Royal College of Surgeons. The basic Royal College diplomas
entitling a person to practise medicine and surgery in the UK,
where, curiously enough, medically qualified doctors are also
entitled to practise dentistry. However, without a dental
degree, no one does.

MB, BS (MB,   Bachelor of Medicine, Bachelor of Surgery. The basic
ChB)   University qualifications in the UK to practise medicine and
surgery. Qualified practitioners of medicine (physicians) are
by convention called 'doctor' even if they do not have a
doctoral degree. Surgeons in the UK are distinguished by being
called Mr, Mrs, Miss, etc. In North America the practitioners
of all the branches of medicine are called 'doctor', which is not
a courtesy title, because their qualifying degree is a doctorate.

MD   Doctor of Medicine.
1. In North America this is the basic qualification to practise
medicine and surgery.
2. In the UK and Commonwealth this is a postgraduate degree
given for original research – the medical equivalent of PhD.

What the letters after dentists' names mean

MDS
(MDSc,
MDentSc)
Master of Dental Surgery (or Science). A postgraduate degree which many Universities award for further studies in dental subjects.

MGDS RSC
Eng
Member in General Dental Surgery of the Royal College of Surgeons of England. A diploma given for postgraduate experience and knowledge of general dentistry.

MRCP
Member of the Royal College of Physicians. The equivalent in Medicine of the FRCS. Few dentists have this.

MRCPath
Member of the Royal College of Pathologists. A diploma indicating specialist training in pathology. Some dentists who specialize in oral pathology have this.

MPhil
Master of Philosophy. A research degree intermediate in status between MSc and PhD.

MSc (MS in
N. America)
Master of Science. A postgraduate degree indicating further training in a science subject.

PhD
Doctor of Philosophy. A postgraduate degree for research which may have been in any subject at a University, not necessarily dental, though usually so with dentists.

F. Where To Get More Information

The most obvious first point of enquiry may be your dentist. If you don't have a dentist or if you require an independent source of information, the following addresses should be able to help.

AUSTRALIA

Dental Health Foundation of Australia
(Mr. J.M. Wooley)
University of Sydney, Sydney, NSW 2006.
Tel. 02-660 8808, 02-692 3219

CANADA

Adviser, Dental Health Standards
Health Services and Promotion Branch
Department of National Health and Welfare
Ottawa, K1A 1B4
Tel. (613) 992 6795

This department of Health & Welfare will provide information on request, some publications, and also redirect enquiries to the pertinent authorities.

Canadian Dental Association
1815 Alta Vista Drive
Ottawa, K1G 3Y6
Tel. (613) 523 1770

This is the professional association for dentists in Canada, and will provide certain information on dental health matters, procedures etc.

Also in Canada there are Community Health Centres and Public Health Centres in various locations, which will provide information. See your local phone book.

HONG KONG

Dental Health Committee
Hong Kong Dental Association
Duke of Windsor Social Service Building
8th floor, 15 Hennessey Road
Hong Kong
Tel. 5–285 327

This organization will provide information on dental health and answer questions by letter or telephone in both Cantonese and English.

JAPAN

At present there appears to be no organization undertaking to provide information on dental health matters to members of the public in Japanese or in English.

NEW ZEALAND

New Zealand Dental Health Foundation
(Mrs M. Mortensen)
P.O. Box 28086, Aukland.

REPUBLIC OF IRELAND

The Dental Health Foundation
29 Kenilworth Square
Dublin 6
Tel. Dublin 97 89 21

An independent organization set up to improve the dental health of Irish people. It will provide information by letter or over the phone on all aspects of dental health.

UNITED KINGDOM

British Dental Health Foundation

Kingston House,
7 London Road,
Old Stratford, Milton Keynes MK19 6AE.
Tel. (0908) 567614/567639

An independent charity set up to improve the dental health of British people. It will provide information by letter or over the phone on all aspects of dental health.

Community Health Councils

(see local phone book)

A kind of health equivalent of the citizen's advice bureau, set up to represent to official bodies consumers' views on the health care they are getting, and to give advice on obtaining treatment under the National Health Service, complaints procedures and so on.

Family Practitioners Committee

(see phone book under local District Health Authority)

A body which handles the contracts and pays fees to dentists (and doctors) within the Health District. In addition they keep lists of dentists in that District, advise on charges, and in some cases keep lists of dentists prepared to provide dentures, or treat mildly handicapped people under the National Health Service. This is the body to which the public may complain about dental and medical services.

District Health Education Services

(see phone book under local District Health Authority)

Teams of people trained to give health education, having access to film and other audio-visual aids. They organize health education projects in schools, clinics, and elsewhere.

Fluoridation Society
64 Wimpole Street,
London W1 8AL
Tel. 01-486 7007

National Anti-fluoridation Campaign
P. Clavell-Blount,
36 Station Road,
Thames Ditton, Surrey KT7 0NS
Tel. 01-398 2117

National Pure Water Association (also against fluoridation)
213 Withington Road,
Manchester M16 8NB

The following organizations have leaflets and other materials on dental health, but do not have an advisory service:

Health Education Council
78 New Oxford Street, London WC1A 1AH
Tel. 01-637 1881

Gibbs Oral Hygiene Service
Hesketh House, Portman Square,
London W1A 1DY

General Dental Council
37 Wimpole Street,
London W1

UNITED STATES OF AMERICA

I am informed that there is no organization independent of the dental profession which provides information on dental matters in the USA. However, the American Dental Association itself has facilities for answering enquiries.

American Dental Association
211 E. Chicago Avenue
Chicago, Ill. 60611
Tel. (312) 440 2500

Index

Page numbers in **bold type** refer to main sections; those in *italic* refer to pages with illustrations

186

Index

Index

isoglucose 68
isomalt (Palatinit®) 50, 58, **61**

jacket crown 175

katemfe fruit 64

labelling on food products 37,
  67–8
lactobiose 49, **52**
lactose 49, **52**
laevulose 49, **51–2**
laxative effect of polyols (osmotic
  diarrhoea) 59, 60
ledges (overhangs) 84, **86**, 127, 134
levulose 49, **51–2**
licensing of food additives 61, 64,
  65, 67
lining material 175
low-calorie drinks 48, 62, 63, 64,
  67, 158
Lycasins® 49, **54**

maltose 53
mannitol 50, 58, **59**, 61
maple syrup **53**
marathon runners 55
matrix band 175
meat, sugar contents of 159
medicines, sugar-free 161–72
milk and milk products, sugar
  contents of 161
milk sugar (lactose) 49, **52**
mints (peppermints) 45
miracle fruit 66
miraculin 66
mixtures of sweeteners **66–7**
molar teeth 92, 119, 131
molasses 50
molasses sugar 50
monellin 66
monosaccharide 68
mottling of enamel 18, 104, 108,
  113, 114, 115
mouth guards 138
mouth mirrors **73–5**
mouthwashes **101–2**
muscovado sugar 50
mutanase 29

neohesperidin dihydrochalcone
  (neoDHC) 66
Newbrun, Ernest 110
non-nutritive sweeteners **61–6**
non-sugar sweeteners 45, 49–**50**,
  58–67

obesity 32, 34, 47
oral hygiene 175
oral surgeon 178
orthodontic checks **135–6**
orthodontic retainers 136
orthodontic treatment 132, 134,
  136–7
orthodontist 178
osmotic diarrhoea 59, 60
overhangs (of fillings) 84, **86**, 127,
  134, 175

Palatinit® 50, 58, **61**
parental conditioning by
  children 34–5
Parkinson's disease and saliva
  flow 25
pastries, sugar contents of 156
pedodontist 179
peppermints 45
periodontal bone loss 124, 125,
  128, 129–30
periodontal pocket 123–5, 134
periodontist 179
pH changes on the tooth
  surface 42–4, 47
phenylketonuria (PKU) 62–3
physical contact with children 89,
  91, 93
PKU (phenylketonuria) 62–3
plaque **10–13**, 22, 47, 122–7, 175
  bacteria changed by low sugar
    frequency 52
  -disclosing dyes **69–70**, 77
  and gum disease **122–7**
  removal **69–94**
  variation 13
pocket (periodontal pocket) 175
post crown 175

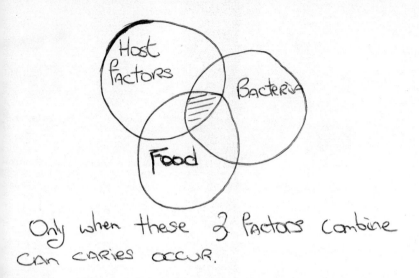

Only when these 3 factors combine
can caries occur.